Expert Witness Training

Profit from your Expertise

By Judd Robbins

Judd Robbins

Expert Witness Training

Copyright

For further information or permissions, contact the publisher:

Presentation Dynamics
2305-C Ashland Street #437
Ashland, OR 97520
Voice Mail and Fax: 949-666-5030
www.expert-witnesses.net

http://www.expert-witnesses.net

ISBN # 978-1-928564-22-5
LCCN # 2009909573
Fonts used: Calibri for body text; Cambria for headings

To Albert Einstein

For motivation, inspiration, and imagination

And to my current, past, and extended family members
who have been by my side and in my heart
for so many years and in so many endeavors

Special thanks to:

Teresa Cutler-Broyles – *Editor-in-Chief*
InkWell International, www.inkwell-inc.biz

Robert Edwards – *Legal Review*
Professor, State University of New York at Canton

Allen R. Hicks – *Cover Design*

And more thanks to friends and family who contributed
advice and support in areas of editing, proofreading,
structure, title, and marketing:

Steven Hersch, Lin Van Heuit-Robbins, Susan Saladoff,
JoAnn Weisel, and Lee Weisel

Disclaimer

This Expert Witness Training book is for information only. The data and information contained within is based on information from various published and unpublished sources and merely represents general training and opinions of the author Judd Robbins. Care has been taken to confirm the accuracy of all information contained within, but much of this information is based on the personal experiences and opinions of Judd Robbins. The author and publisher are not responsible for errors or omissions or for any consequences from application of the information in this educational product. Neither Presentation Dynamics nor Judd Robbins makes any guarantees or warranties, express or implied, regarding the currentness, completeness, or legal accuracy of any information within this training book for any particular purpose. This book is not intended to offer legal advice, is not intended to be state-specific, and is not intended to replace legal advice or common sense in any legal setting. You are expected to make your own professional decisions regarding your conduct as an expert witness, intelligently using the advice, guidance, and experience of the author.

Choice of Words

Men v. Women - Throughout this book, I make conscious efforts to respect the fact that attorneys are sometimes men and sometimes women, and so are expert witnesses. Authors often struggle with the desire to use "his or her" pronoun references, as opposed to simply "his" all the time, or "her" all the time. I have chosen to use all three approaches at various times during the book. Whoever you are, I have thought of you in my writings, and hope that you will recognize my efforts to surmount these potential word problems.

Attorney v. Retaining Attorney - A similar problem arises in referring to the attorneys who may hire you as an expert witness. In real life, the attorney who hires (retains) you as an expert is most often referred to as "your attorney", although "retaining attorney" might be more accurate. Since they may hire you, but in fact be considered as a 'client' of yours, it might be equally accurate to refer to them as "your attorney-client". Either of these longer phrases might be arguably more accurate, but after significant consideration, I have decided not to bog down the text of this book with them. I've used them from time to time to satisfy some readers who want the greater accuracy, and other readers who don't want the expert to sound like a 'hired gun'.

Criminal v. Civil — As an expert witness, you will have the experience of helping clients in both criminal and civil cases. The laws as well as the legal procedures are different. The side that brings the case is called the plaintiff in a civil case and the prosecution in a criminal case. The attorney representing the plaintiff in a civil case is called the plaintiff or the plaintiff's attorney. The attorney representing the prosecution in a criminal matter is called the prosecutor. Throughout most of this book, I refer to the plaintiff and the defense sides. Your work as an expert witness is virtually identical in either so I have chosen not to muddy up the text by trying to use both terms *plaintiff* and *prosecution* when discussing the side that brings a case.

Contents

5

LESSON 4: WORKING WITH ATTORNEYS 79

LESSON 5: CONDUCTING AN EXPERT INVESTIGATION

.... 97

LESSON 9: FREQUENTLY ASKED TESTIMONIAL QUESTIONS 175

Introduction

Profit from your expertise; become an expert witness and become qualified to testify in a court of law.

My name is Judd Robbins. I have been a testifying expert and an expert consultant for lawyers across the U.S. and abroad since 1986. In the twenty years before that, I was a specialist in computers. The transition from being an expert in my specialty, to being an expert qualified to testify in a court of law, has been rewarding in personal, professional, and financial ways.

These twelve lessons cover what I've learned from personal and professional studies and my experience with attorneys, their clients, judges, juries and nail biting testimony in courtrooms. My testimonial experience ranges from murder to fraud to divorce to airplane crashes. Litigation in the United States is widespread, and crimes themselves span a host of disciplines. Expert witnesses and consultants, and especially those with skills in the legal arena, are always in demand. A fee of $300 to $400 an hour is commonplace; this can range up to $1000 an hour if you are a medical expert.

That being said, don't give up your day job. That 'day job' is where you gained the experience that may qualify you to be an expert witness. The attorneys and the courts expect that you will remain current in your profession, that you practice what you preach, and that your time as an expert witness is a sideline and not your only professional activity. Experts often view their witness experience as simply a well-paying moonlighting job. Continuing to work in your specialty lends credibility and substance to your occasional engagements as an expert consultant or witness.

For me, witness work contains the novel element of performance art. As you might suspect, it requires speaking skills, teaching skills, and self-confidence. If you already have those skills plus expertise in your specialty, you're only one step away from being an expert witness. If you have only one or two of those capabilities, you're still well ahead of the game. And even if you have none of those skills yet, you can still parlay your expertise in your discipline into this rewarding new arena.

Seminars and workshops exist to teach professionals how to speak in public. Schools exist that specialize in training teachers. You can always study and improve, and then apply those skills in your expert witness career. I designed this course, 'Expert Witness Training,' to teach you about the exciting arena of expert witnessing, and how to prepare for and perform in it. You'll learn how to conduct an expert investigation, prepare an expert report, work with attorneys, and testify in depositions and in courtrooms.

Should you become an expert witness in your specialty? Can you? This course will help you come to the best decision. If you've already made the decision to become an expert witness but have not yet been successful at attracting lawyers to retain you, I can share my experience about ways to connect with hiring attorneys. Maybe you are a successful expert witness already, and you'd like to learn how to improve on that success. Perhaps you'd like to be called as an expert more often, and to reap the rewards for your improved skills.

The lessons taught in this book have been learned and applied by me over decades. In hours, you can learn how to avoid mistakes that took me months or years to discover. You might still make errors, but you will improve with each case and attorneys will hire you back and pass your name around to other attorneys who need experts. Expert witnessing is an energizing arena and if you have the attitude, aptitude, and fortitude, you will receive respect, personal satisfaction, and increased pay.

Expert Consultants versus Expert Witnesses

The prospect of being an 'expert witness' and testifying in court is exciting to many professionals. However, roughly 90% of the time, even if you are hired to be an expert witness, you will act instead as an expert consultant because the vast majority of cases simply do not go to trial.

The expert consultant role is often filled by a specialist who is eventually designated as the expert witness. The consultant role combines teaching and analytical roles that are equivalent to those of an expert witness, except that they do not include testifying in court. If you're already an expert in your profession, you can use the lessons in this book to learn how best to find new expert witness jobs and how to master this discipline. This form of consulting spans the following:

Investigation – You study the technical details of materials, accidents, or other events. You might run tests, create reconstructions, or research books and journals for writings on the same subject matter as your case. Afterward, you consolidate your research, analyze your findings, and draw conclusions from them. Your primary role in the beginning stage of an investigation is to learn the technical facts of the case and to explain to your retaining attorney the application of those facts. This, in turn, will guide your retaining attorney to better decisions.

Assessment -- Attorneys will sometimes hire you to assess the technical merits of the other side's claims. You may review their submissions and give your opinions about the bases of the claims and their potential strengths or weaknesses.

Opinions --- As an expert consultant, you generally act behind the scenes. The other side in the case won't even realize you exist. That is the way it will stay if your analyses and assessments suggest to your retaining attorney that his case is weak, or if the attorney chooses not to go to trial because he simply wants to use your technical analyses to extract the best deal or settlement for his client.

Attorneys will have a deadline by which time they have to 'designate,' or officially identify, their expert witness. The 'discovery' process covers the preliminary phase of every legal matter. This is when investigations are performed and appropriate information is shared among the parties. If the attorneys like your results, and are comfortable with and confident of you, they may formally designate you to the other side as their expert witness. You continue to be responsible for any ongoing investigations, analyses, and assessments, but you now will add the center stage role of potentially testifying in depositions or at trial. You will have to follow stringent rules for investigations, evaluations, and reporting on results and opinions.

In cases that involve higher stakes, attorneys will sometimes hire separate specialists to serve as expert consultants and expert witnesses. If you are hired in one of these roles, you may or may not have contact with the person hired to fill the other. Attorneys are taught to keep their expert consultants and witnesses separated but in my experience, they do not know or follow this advice. If you become one of two experts (an expert consultant or an expert witness) in a case, ask your attorney about the possible upside or downside of having conversations with the other expert.

Understanding the Written and Unwritten Rules

You must know the rules, like Rule 702 of the Federal Rules of Evidence, which lists the requirements for serving as an expert witness, and Rule 706, which governs being a court-appointed expert. I'll explain these and also tell you about the unwritten, even unspoken rules, the metaphorical elbows that can be thrown at your head during testimony and that can shake your confidence or distract you from the true intent of the questions. You'll learn about the equivalent of sucker punches that appear as trick questions that can disqualify you and your testimony, and these lessons will show you how to play your position on a team as an expert witness.

In essence, these lessons will teach you in advance what you can expect from the other players on the team. Your client pays you to know this game; it's not acceptable to learn the rules as you play. The sooner you learn the game, the better you will perform and the better your reputation.

Entering the World of Expert Witnessing

You can certainly become an expert witness on your own without this program, but learning these skills will help you move into that arena more quickly and successfully, leading to your being hired again. I offer you a complete overview with tips and tricks for becoming and being an expert witness, and you will know whether you're ready to join the expert witness ranks or whether you need to enhance your expert witness skills.

1

Stepping into the Legal Game

In various legal settings, from courts to arbitrations and mediations, any person who has relevant "knowledge, skill, experience, training, or education" may qualify to testify as an expert. However, a successful expert witness has to know more than just his or her own area of expertise.

Understanding the Overall Legal Framework

You can find that quotation about "knowledge, skill, experience, training or education" in Rule 702 in the Federal Rules of Evidence. The rule also specifies that the expert witness has to apply that knowledge and those skills in ways to qualify both you as the expert and your work. First, you must base your testimony on "sufficient facts or data." As an expert witness, you have to convince the court that those facts provide a solid basis for your opinions. You may not just rely on instincts or your experience in the industry.

Federal Rule of Evidence 702 and the Daubert Guideline

You must determine what set of facts and data will support any conclusions reached. To guide you, Rule 702 adds that your testimony must be "the product of reliable principles and methods." As an expert in the field, you should already be familiar with the principles and methods used by others in your field. Be prepared to reference and explain any commonly accepted rules, standards, or guidelines that govern your industry. Finally, the rule dictates that you have to have "applied the principles and methods reliably to the facts of the case."

The current wording in Rule 702 of the Federal Rules of Evidence regarding "testimony by experts" has its origins in the rulings from three well-known legal cases: Daubert v. Merrill Dow Pharmaceuticals in 1993, General Electric v. Joiner in 1997, and Kumho Tire v. Carmichael in 1999. You will hear the name *Daubert* frequently when speaking with attorneys.

Attorneys must anticipate the standards imposed by *Daubert* when they select expert witnesses in support of their cases.

TACTIC: Understanding Daubert and its implications on your performance as an expert increases your chances that attorneys will hire you.

You, and the attorneys with whom you work, must anticipate legal challenges to the acceptability of investigations and analyses. Daubert standards and challenges guide what you, as an expert witness, must understand and how you should conduct your investigations, testing, and analyses.

The Expert Witness as part of a Team

Competitive sports have sides – one opponent against another opponent. Lawyers admit that the judicial arena is also adversarial; while a trial is not a game, gamesmanship is involved. You can play in a pickup game, but it takes advanced skills to play in the major leagues. No matter what your specialty, becoming an expert witness in your specialty is the 'major leagues' for you.

It's not about a good team or a bad team, a right team or a wrong team, but there are always sides. Each side wants to win, and sometimes a weaker side wins. In the legal arena, lawsuits involve at least one plaintiff and one defendant. The jurors or the judge often rely on experts to help explain and clarify complicated facts. A 'bench trial' occurs when a trial has no jurors and the judge delivers the final verdict.

Two Sides

You could be hired by either the defense or the plaintiff/prosecution. In criminal cases, the 'prosecution' is the party that brings the lawsuit; in civil cases, the 'plaintiff' is the party that brings the lawsuit. I'll refer to plaintiffs throughout rather than complicate the text.

TACTIC: Judges tend to look favorably on experts who show a balanced approach to litigation support.

Always working for defense attorneys or for plaintiff attorneys suggests bias, and I have found that attorneys perceive me as objective because I've worked on both sides of cases. This, in turn, has led to more casework. If you choose to always work for one side or the other, even for what seem to be good reasons, doing so will restrict your choices and your future work. As an expert witness, you can offer objective analytical skills to attorneys on both sides of any case.

A good thing to remember as an expert witness is, as defense attorneys say, all defendants are entitled to a legal defense and are innocent until proven guilty. You do not resolve the right or wrong of a case. You bring your expertise and knowledge to the court, present your analysis and findings, and then provide impartial testimony.

Legal Settings beyond the Courtroom

Attorneys retain experts in three principal legal settings: courtroom trials, mediations, and arbitrations. In mediations and arbitrations, a lawyer, judge or retired judge works to negotiate a compromise. In arbitrations, the parties may agree in advance to accept the arbitrator's findings as binding.

The lessons in this book rely on my experience in courts and in litigations that often led to a courtroom trial. However, my advice on preparation and presentation, as well as the tips and techniques for giving testimony, apply to each of the three possible settings.

You can offer your expert services in any of these settings.[1]

Lawyers Need Experts

The need for expert witnesses spans subjects from A to Z. Lawyers use experts in litigation from medical malpractice to engineering to accounting to the ubiquitous field of computing. Internet

---

[1] If offering testimony in mediations or arbitrations appeals to you as a way to expand your business, then you can consider contacting mediation or arbitration service organizations. Let them know of your availability to work with them as a specialist in your field of expertise.

resources list over 500 categories and thousands of subcategories, ranging from abuse to zoning; your specialty probably falls somewhere in the list. You can see a list of principal consulting categories in the Registry of Experts at expert-witnesses.net.

You must bring to the table pre-existing expertise that includes detailed knowledge in your subject. You may have already published books, articles, or journal treatises. You may already consult independently, or you may work for a company as a specialist. If you also bring the skill of communication, you can help the litigants reach an out-of-court settlement. The basic question about your qualifications remains: Can you legitimately present yourself to attorneys as a possible expert witness?

Why Do Lawyers Need You?

Attorneys know the law but rarely will they know your specialty area. Since they cannot testify even if they do understand the field, they have to hire experts like you. Additionally, lawyers do not have the time to do the research and analysis to obtain the technical nitty-gritty about the case, so they hire you to spend your time doing that. You know how to do the research and the follow-on analyses. When litigants dispute the same evidence, and either side might win the case, then you can testify about the results.

What evidence you should present during testimony can become an ethical quandary. Defense attorneys must do their best job to thwart the efforts of the other side's attorneys, or play the game well enough to obtain an innocent verdict for their clients. The expert witness must present the technical evidence in the best possible light. At the same time, you may have your own doubts about the strength of the evidence, and you may see the reasonableness of the other side's evidence. Sometimes, you will realize that the person whose side has hired you may have committed the alleged crime.

You must present and explain the helpful evidence as well as possible and leave the so-called harmful evidence to the other expert. It is up to other side's experts to present the harmful information as best as they can.

TACTIC: You can contribute to each case by providing your attorney with analyses of the facts, no matter whether your findings seem helpful or not.

Let the attorney decide for his client whether to proceed with the case or attempt to settle for a better possible result.

The majority of legal disputes never reach the stage of a trial. Once everyone discovers the facts, the experts complete the technical analyses, and the lawyers take the depositions, the outcome often becomes evident. The parties can use your work as an expert as the basis for an eventual settlement. Sometimes, attorneys will hire you as an expert to provide them with these analyses before they even file a lawsuit. Your objective interpretation of the information can sometimes convince the attorney against filing the lawsuit. In the same fashion, even after filing a lawsuit, plaintiffs may drop a case if an expert's analysis shows that they will lose. When an expert for the defense shows why their side will lose, that is when talks for the best settlement or plea bargain begin.

As a plaintiff's expert, you may find information that sustains the allegations. As a defendant's or plaintiff's expert, you may find 'exculpatory' evidence that helps to reduce or negate the charges. The defense can use this additional information to support arguments in court against conviction. Your information may not lead directly to a verdict in favor of your side, but it may lead to a better settlement.

Ethical quandaries can emerge for you when presenting exculpatory evidence for the defense, or weak evidence for the plaintiff. If you wish to avoid these difficulties, you'll simply have to choose your cases differently.

Who is an Expert?

Do you know if standards and accreditations exist in your field? Do you meet the standards in your field as an expert? Did you obtain available accreditations in your specialty? Did you earn the license required in your specialty? Did you obtain expected and available certifications in your specialty? Consider additional work to prepare yourself. Lawyers and the courts they serve want expert witnesses to look good on paper, sound good in court, and legitimately have the qualifications to be there.

You will hear the term 'admissibility.' A judge determines whether to 'admit' you, your credentials, and your work into the court. The judge has the 'gatekeeper' role and decides whether to allow you to present your work and your opinions in the courtroom. The opposing attorney may successfully present legal reasons why the judge should not admit your work into evidence. Inadmissibility may not indicate that your work was poor, but it does declare that your work did not meet legal standards. This can be a damaging loss to your side and a great victory for the other side, and will successfully keep your work from ever being considered by the jurors.

Your retaining attorney has to deal with legal considerations regarding admissibility. However, you can help provide your opinion with a solid foundation by performing your work carefully, preparing it to meet standards, and presenting it well. You cannot scrimp on care, and your work must meet the norms and standards of your industry. If you express an opinion that seems straightforward to you, it still may sound ridiculous in court if you based it on incomplete, poorly documented, or otherwise shoddy procedures.

What Does Your Job History Say About You?

A combination of regulatory agency, academic, and industry experience will strongly support you in your role as an expert witness.

Academic experience alone, without hands-on work, can seem only theoretical and may lead to rigorous cross examination. Attorneys may capitalize on this weakness by presenting hypothetical questions that can be difficult during testimony because of your lack of real-world experience. Lack of industry experience can come across as 'ivory tower syndrome,' a weakness found often in academic expert witnesses. Jurors may find you less believable and your opinions less acceptable.

Extensive industry experience will help you most when making a transition from just an industry expert to a litigation consultant. Jurors will easily recognize your expertise if they learn that you have worked as an industry expert for years. Attorneys will then find it difficult to discredit your credentials.

If you have worked for a law enforcement agency or governmental commission, at the state or federal level, you may have a built-in acceptability to jurors. While some jurors may have a bias against you because you worked for the government, government employ does bring a notable credential to the table on your behalf.

Taking a Long-Term Perspective to Litigation Support

Whether an independent consultant or an employee of a company, the expert witness must still act as a team player. You will work with at least one attorney on each case. You will meet with the client, or colleagues of the client. You will meet a host of other support personnel and other experts who were retained to help with portions of the case. Bring your expertise to the table, but also bring the same charm, smile, warmth, and friendliness that you show to a jury and judge.

Remember that you may have expert witness work as a side job for decades, not just one or two times. If you are useful to your retaining attorney, your first case will turn into your tenth or your 100th. Maintaining your expertise and staying current in your field is vitally important. This includes attending conferences and seminars, reading appropriate journals, books, and other treatises published in your field, and staying aware of the latest developments.

Explaining Legal Jargon

You will need to understand many new terms specific to the legal world. For an extensive list, see Appendix A.

Generally, you should understand the meaning of 'privilege' in the United States. Privilege protects conversations between attorneys and their clients. 'Attorney-client privilege' exists in the law to foster open communication between clients and their attorneys. Because neither the attorney nor the client has to reveal the content of their discussions to the other side, they can both feel freer to have honest discussions with each other. You, on the other hand, are not a client so what you say or write to your retaining attorney about a case does not have this protection under the law.

The laws on privilege vary among the states, and at times may even vary between state and federal courts. When an attorney retains you, have a discussion about privilege. Understand privilege fully as it covers communications, both written and oral, between you and the attorney. You do not want to become a liability to your attorney or his client if an opposing attorney asks you about what you knew, know, or said.

Attorneys may hire you as an expert to help them in either civil or criminal cases; the rules of law differ. Ask the attorney retaining you to explain the laws involved and how your opinion and work will tie in to any relevant law. Criminal cases often end in a jail term, while civil cases often end with a financial judgment. An expert witness serves the same role of objective expert in both styles of case. You have to analyze and explain facts in such a way that you help the lawyers to do their job and help the court to determine the final verdict.

In contrast to an expert witness, a 'lay witness' or 'fact witness' is any individual who actually testifies and who has firsthand knowledge of events from directly seeing or hearing them. As the expert witness, you will look at material, interview individuals or reconstruct events, and then testify about what likely occurred.

Your expertise, combined with careful and methodical work, qualifies you to present an opinion about an event that happened when you weren't even there. The court does not have to accept or believe what you say. You must convince the jurors or the judge of the believability of what you say because of your expertise and workmanship.

Writing a Contract for your Services

Explain what services you offer and your fees for them. I use a simple one-page combination of contract and fee schedule, included as Appendix E. This contract defines the terms of the retainer agreement and handles any disputes. Feel free to use it and change it with your name and information. Preferably, have the retaining attorney sign it for his law firm, along with the client or case name. If your retention is for the defense, or in a case involving criminal conduct, you should definitely sign a contract with a law firm as opposed to the actual defendant.

TACTIC: If a client pays you directly with illegally obtained money, you may have to return the money.

From time to time, an attorney will say that his law firm has its own contract or letter of engagement that they want you to sign. Read through it and suggest any changes you would like. Generally, they will make any requested changes before you both sign the contract.

I combine my contract with my simple fee schedule because I want it known that I expect to receive payment for specific tasks in advance. For example, experts often require advance payment for deposition and trial testimonial time; additionally, the research and analysis that precede the writing of an expert report can consume a non-trivial amount of time and money as well and asking for an upfront fee is acceptable.[2]

What happens if you do not receive payment in advance? How likely is it that you'll receive payment? Why should you even wonder? If a case ends poorly for your client, and you did not receive payment in advance for that final testimonial day, you may have a reluctant client or an unhappy law firm. Sometimes, the clients hiring you have to borrow money to pay an attorney, who then tells the client that he or she must also hire an expert. Understand this and you can appreciate the client's plight. However, unless you volunteer your expert witness services, you

---

[2] Your expert report delivers your opinions, your research, and the bases for your opinions. Rule 26 in the Federal Rules of Civil Procedure (FRCP) requires you to include the information that you considered in reaching your conclusions or opinions. I'll explain in detail what you must know about this rule in Lesson 6, "Writing an Expert Report." For now, know that if your expert conclusions do **not** work well for the attorney, he or she may decide not to use you any longer as an expert witness. See Appendix C for the actual wording of Rule 26.

should still protect yourself by ensuring that they pay you, at least in the form of a starting retainer.

You should definitely ask for advance payment for significant work, but do not ignore reality. Sometimes you will have to be pragmatic and work first, and then ask for the money by invoice afterwards. I did it that way earlier in my career and, most of the time, the lawyers or their clients did pay. More information about contracts and fees can be found in Lesson 2.

The Intricacies of Client Selection

Attorneys can choose experts, but experts can also exercise selectivity about who becomes a client. Many factors go into making that decision.

You have to anticipate how weak or strong you will be when an opposing attorney uses techniques that diminish your credentials and tears you down. He may attack the credibility of what you say, or have said, or have written and published. Knowing in advance what techniques an opposing attorney may employ to attack your credibility should help you decide whether to take a case.

If you accept an assignment as a defendant's expert witness, the other side may tie you in personally or emotionally to the crime. You may be disparaged as sympathetic to causes or groups simply by association. And if you are an expert who never takes defense cases, you can expect that the attorney will attack your bias toward plaintiffs. These verbal attacks attempt to undermine your credibility with the jury.

Before you take a case, consider that your client may be right or wrong, innocent or guilty. Attorneys do not always know if they have an innocent or guilty client until they learn about the case during the discovery phase; neither will you. You have to perform your analyses objectively and apply your expertise to whatever you discover. Can you perform professionally regardless of the findings?

TACTIC: Sometimes, you will be helping a guilty party. You may not feel good about that, so just focus on feeling good about the work you do.

You should select your cases based on your qualifications, the integrity and stability of the client or law firm, or simply the interest you have in the subject matter. If you do choose cases based on ethical reasons, or other personal issues, you should not advertise any bias you use; if you do, you risk being characterized as 'not objective' in front of a jury.

Generally, lawyers contact you because your CV underscores your expertise in the subject matter of their case. CV stands for Curriculum Vitae and is also known as a résumé. Attorneys prefer to call it a CV, so I will do so throughout the book. In the initial conversation you can determine whether your qualifications fit the specifics of the case. Assess the breadth of your knowledge of the subject, your ability to face possible challenges in court, and the time it will take to do the job.

It will frustrate you and damage your reputation if you could have done the job well but simply didn't have the time to do it right. Do not take on a case unless you are confident that you will have the time and energy to pursue the case fully. This includes:

- Completing required tasks

- Preparing a thorough report

- Attending meetings

- Participating in phone calls

- Travel time

- Testifying in deposition and trials

First Contacts with Attorneys and Clients

Your first contact with potential clients will come from the client or his/her attorney. Sometimes an attorney may call to check on your availability, interest, and relevant qualifications. The lawyer may have gotten your name from a colleague, or simply looked you up on the Internet and found you listed on your own website or on an Internet-based registry of expert witnesses. Sometimes, the preliminary phone call will come from a prospective client (plaintiff or defendant) who is simply taking a more hands-on approach to expert witness selection.

When someone calls, write down the date and ask the attorney or potential client's complete name and its proper spelling. Ask for their phone number. Take notes about the case as you chat, but not extensive or compromising notes. For example, an indiscreet attorney might say: "My client's guilty but I want to get him the best possible deal." Do not write those sorts of remarks down; the notes taken during that first phone call can become the first entry in a file folder in which you keep all notes and records for the case. Your notes and that indiscreet remark may become evidence that you might have to turn over.[3] All the materials you review over the course of a case constitute your 'file folder.'[45]

---

[3] Guilt or innocence remains the jurisdiction of a judge and/or a jury.

[4] You may receive email from attorneys that contains information about their clients. Honesty and ethics require you to keep records of all email communications, including those you think the client or attorney should never *(Continued on next page)* →

Initial contact with attorneys can also happen through email or fax. In any case, be prepared to give references. Sending an email or a fax may seem an impersonal first contact, but it does save an attorney time. Be aware that if they are contacting you, they are probably contacting other potential experts as well. Respond quickly to the email, and then follow up with a phone call within twenty four hours.

It may be a paralegal or investigator who initiates the first contact. It is best to ask directly if the caller is an attorney or holds another position on the case. If the attorney eventually does hire you to help with the case, your records should reflect the date you were first contacted, and by whom.

Assessing the Case

Far too often, the person contacting you will describe elements of the case, then ask you "what you think" or whether "you're interested in the case." At that point, neither one of you knows the answer so you should not try to provide one. Both parties need to ask additional questions before you agree to take on a

---

have sent to you. Throwing away communications may constitute destruction of evidence.

[5] If you have to organize voluminous records or files, label the boxes or the piles appropriately for the case, and include the attorney's name, phone number and case identifier on the outside or on the tab. You should add the attorney's number to your cell phone contact list. When the case completes, or you withdraw, include final notes about how the case ended. If it ended in your withdrawal, note your reasons for the withdrawal. The attorney may ask you to return the materials that you reviewed, or sometimes to destroy them. Add a note to your file folder about the disposition of the evidence.

case and/or they agree to hire you. One good question that rarely gets asked is "what are you trying to accomplish and how can I help you?" It may surprise you how much you can help once you know the attorney's legal goals

Attorneys always ask about possible conflicts of interest. Any pre-existing relationship with a person, persons, or firm involved in a case constitutes a conflict of interest. This kind of conflict, and conflicts of time, are often unfortunate reasons you are not able to take a case.

Make sure you ask about any known scheduling for the case:

- Are there firm dates?

- Are they flexible?

- Are there dates for the close of discovery?

- Are depositions already underway or scheduled?

- Is there a trial date?

- What is the projected duration of the trial?

The job of an expert witness is a demanding and sometimes grueling exercise. Ideally, you want to take on cases that are satisfying and rewarding. If you like your expert witness work, you will have your heart in it and you will be a better witness.

What if you decide to reject a case?

The biggest and first reason you should reject a case is if, in good conscience, you do not think that you are qualified. You may not believe that you have the appropriate experience and skills to do the investigation, analysis, or tests for the case. Since you will eventually have to defend any opinions you form from your work, you should be confident that you have the right credentials and skills for doing that work. On the other hand, you just might not like the sound of the attorney on the other end of the line. You might not like his attitude, or you might conclude a lack of professionalism in his approach to the case.

I once had an attorney call me with one month notice to ask me to perform the entire investigation, analysis, and writing of the report. A month may sound reasonable, but on further questioning I discovered that the opposing counsel had hired their expert a year earlier and the expert had been working on the report for nearly 9 months before finally completing it. Needless to say, I would not have been able to do as competent a job within a month. If you do not have the time to do the job properly, you will suffer when you are unable to present a credible expert analysis or a defensible expert testimony.

TACTIC: Do not accept a case with a timeline so tight that you will not have time to do the job right.

You may reject a case if you truly have ethical or moral issues with it. I know expert witnesses who do not accept any defense cases having to do with child pornography. Some expert witness's certifying organizations forbid members from taking on any defense cases. Some expert witnesses will not take on a case if they think their side will lose. They simply do not want their own reputation hurt by a losing verdict.

You are more likely to be on the losing side of a case if you work with attorneys who are dishonest or incompetent. You might become suspicious if attorneys are unresponsive to your questions or needs in the case. When attorneys discount the importance of steps you suggest, or documents that you feel should be considered, suspect a problem. Sometimes, you can only confirm your suspicions after the case ends and after the clients sue the attorney for malpractice.

However, you can check the reputation of virtually every attorney in the country before you accept a case. The Martindale-Hubbell® Peer Review Ratings™ offers a service for any person seeking to hire an attorney. You can use this service to help you determine whether an attorney is ethical and has a good track record. On the Internet, look up 'peer review ratings service' at Martindale.com.

TACTIC: To learn about the performance track record of attorneys, use the 'peer review ratings service' at Martindale.com

Various reasons exist for rejecting cases and you can always express your rejection politely. It is a good idea to keep a list of names and contact information of other experts to whom you can refer the clients you must turn down. Referrals to other experts generate goodwill, and may lead to new business from the attorney or the other expert in the future.

Other Litigation Support Roles

The Expert Report is the premier piece of writing you may construct, and Lesson 6 focuses entirely on this. However, you might also write and sign other legal documents, or portions of them. These often take the form of an 'affidavit' or a 'declaration,' explained below, in support of an attorney's legal motion to the court for other purposes in the case.

In the first phases of a case, an attorney may hire you solely as an expert consultant. An expert consultant and an expert witness may have equivalent skills, but attorneys do not have to tell the other side that they have hired an expert consultant, nor do they have to reveal the consultant's work, research, or analyses. Often the consultant becomes the expert witness after the analyses are done. The attorney might designate[6] you as the expert witness if your results favor the client. He also may choose to use the strength of your credentials and work to present the best of the bad evidence.

Regardless of which role you serve, if you are not serving both roles over time, your attorney may ask you to write or agree to sign an affidavit or declaration. In such a document, you testify to the validity of information. You may know this information from your industry knowledge, and it may support the lawyer's motion for summary judgment. It also could support a legal argument for another purpose in the case. Sometimes, the attorney will ask you to write a simple paragraph or page of technical information that he can then merge and submit as part of his legal document. He will ask you to sign that document, thereby certifying that the content is your submission. It is common to help with the creation and submission of these forms, regardless of whether you are an expert witness or an expert consultant.

Summary of Lesson 1

Becoming an expert witness requires that you know your field and know the rules of the legal game. Regardless of whether you are already an expert in your field, you still have to learn and understand what qualifies you to become an acceptable expert witness. You must understand the legal precedents, such as the Daubert case in the Supreme Court, that articulate the approaches you must follow in your litigation support role.

---

[6] Some states do not have expert discovery, so there is no designation. Most states do, however, so the designation process is very common.

Professional and legal qualifications are only the beginning of what an expert witness must offer. Knowing how to relate to attorneys and their clients becomes your next hurdle. Accepting a case puts you at the starting gate; the rest of the track lies just ahead.

2

Money and Ethics

Money and ethics go hand in hand. Before you ever accept your first case, you should prepare a contract to use with attorneys or law firms for your expert witness services. Pricing your consulting services should take several obvious and subtle considerations into account. Later in this lesson I'll offer specific advice on pricing your services but before we explore those bread and butter issues, we should talk about the importance of ethics to your success as an expert witness.

Ethical Considerations

Most of us understand wrong from right. At least, we understand standard societal norms, and that punishments exist for doing things that are wrong. Punishments for unethical conduct as an expert witness can include jail time or fines. Less severe ethical breaches can lead to inadmissible testimony, the loss of your reputation, and the loss of future jobs.

If the side that hired you represents the proverbial 'bad guy,' then your work may help the wrong side, at least from an ethical or moral perspective. You may feel better about helping the right side, but your investigations and analyses should remain the same regardless of the side you represent. Your goal is to determine the pluses and minuses that you learn from your tests or research and inform your retaining attorney. Your investigations and analyses should help guide the attorneys who hired you toward better legal decisions. Let them decide the best way to use your findings.

Frequently, you will not know whose side in a case has more merit until you've reviewed the documents and can come to firm opinions about what has happened. Sometimes, you'll discover that defendants have lied to their attorney. Sometimes, you may discover that a District Attorney has based his prosecution on evidence that a police investigator has misrepresented. In both scenarios, objectively analyzing the technical evidence will enable you to set the attorneys right. In the preliminary phases of the case, your work can help to guide the attorney. Later in the case, your work can help the court to reach a just verdict.

You must be aware of these ethical considerations in your dealings with lawyers and the legal system. The more quickly you recognize ethical pressures, the easier it will be to resist them and become a better expert witness.

TACTIC: Never become an advocate for the side that hires you. Yes, you can help one side or the other, but objectivity has to remain the underlying theme.

Acting Ethically

The expert witness must be an objective contributor to the legal process. You have a responsibility to present technical truths that you discover. If the other side can show that you are not objective, the judge can disallow your testimony and you will have wasted your work and everyone else's time. Leave the advocacy to the attorney; keep the objectivity for you.

So, you may wonder what ethical questions you should consider. How will these questions affect your work as an expert witness?

First, you should not falsify or overstate your credentials. It's likely that opposing counsel will uncover those lies and cast justifiable doubt on the rest of your testimony. Corporate employers are much more lax in checking credentials on a CV than are well-trained lawyers. Clean up your resume, and write the truth. Let your experience lead you to the cases for which you are qualified.

Do not take on a job if it stretches beyond your credentials and competence. Opposing counsel can easily determine when you testify outside the scope of your core expertise. A common result is that the court rejects your status as an expert witness and excludes your testimony.

Finally, you should not even consider an expert witness role if you have any conflicts of interest. For example, it is a conflict if you are working on another, concurrent case for one of the lawyers. It is also a conflict if you have previously discussed details of the case with members of the other side. If you suspect a conflict, discuss it in advance before the attorney hires you.

If no problems exist with a case and you take it on, you will shortly recognize what steps should be undertaken as part of a thorough investigation. Once you identify those steps, you have to take them. You cannot skip steps and say that you did them. You cannot have anyone else do the steps for you, and then say you did them. You cannot change the results of any of the steps. You also cannot insert falsified data into a set of otherwise valid results. Just do what should be done, and do it honestly.

TACTIC: *The judicial system expects you to avoid becoming an advocate for the side that hired you.*

Objectivity and an ethical approach to your work as an expert witness demand that you do the work first and then draw your conclusions afterwards.

Even if your conclusions at the end of your work are the same as your expectations at the beginning, you simply cannot firm up those conclusions before you have a legally defensible basis for drawing them. A cross examining attorney who discovers that you reached a conclusion first, and then justified it and are now testifying to it, may easily diminish the strength of your testimony or even have it stricken from the record.

Do not ignore available and relevant information. Your objectivity must include whatever you discover when working toward your opinions. Otherwise, an attorney can attack your conclusions as false simply because you did not take known facts into account. Likewise, you may not leave out data that you believe will skew the results away from a conclusion that you want to have.

Be careful not to reverse an opinion expressed in previous publications or testimony just because your new attorney wants you to take this new position. If the facts do lead to a different conclusion, you should prepare explanations of the discrepancy between this new opinion and the one previously expressed.

You cannot have a fee schedule that is contingent on a successful outcome in the case. That establishes a bias in your opinions. Using contingent fees is enough to justify the exclusion of your testimony.

Honesty remains paramount. Even though you work with your retaining attorney, do not forget that the attorney is an advocate for the client. You are an objective expert whose job is to investigate and draw conclusions from the facts.

TACTIC: You serve the truth first, and then your own sense of ethics and professionalism. Your objectivity and dedication to truthfulness will serve your client and attorney well and eventually help the court to reach the best verdict.

Having Unethical Things Done to You

Attorneys will sometimes act unethically toward expert witnesses. Sadly, you may experience this with attorneys not only on the opposing side, but with your retaining attorney, as well.

Do not allow your retaining attorney to direct your eventual opinions. Influence can be as blatant as telling you what opinion he wants you to express, or as insidious as showing you only a part of the relevant information in the case. It is possible to become victimized by your retaining attorney if he withholds important data. Be sure to ask if any data exists that you have not yet seen. Don't be shy; in fact, you might as well tell him in the initial conversation that you conduct thorough investigations that must include all relevant information. Ultimately you cannot rely only on information that your retaining attorney tells you. He may wish to influence the basis and foundation on which you draw conclusions and form opinions; therefore you must determine those facts from other sources in your investigation.

Do not give opinions that reach beyond the original scope of engagement. If your attorney subsequently asks you to render additional opinions, be certain to document that request so that you can describe the expansion of your role in the case. Opposing attorneys will often ask you about your original scope of engagement. Keep accurate notes.

When an expert receives payment for services that include expressing an opinion that does not have a solid basis in fact, he is said to 'sell' his opinion. You should not 'sell' your expert opinion, especially if you can tell in advance that you will not have enough time to perform a thorough investigation. Attorneys sometimes wait until late in the case to hire an expert who will offer to say what they want to hear. Again, if you do not have enough time to do the research, you should probably reject the case.

If during questioning you are tired, request a break. Do not fight the fatigue and continue to answer questions. That would be to your detriment. It is your responsibility to ask for a rest if you need one. Remember, opposing lawyers like it when you are uncomfortable.

Lawyers can employ intimidating and abusive techniques. They may repeat questions or wear you down with a series of irrelevant questions. Expect this. Stay calm no matter what techniques they use.

Attorneys for the other side may sometimes ask questions about your private life or your personal habits. Unless these questions relate to your specific expertise in the matter and your competence to offer relevant opinions, your attorney should probably object. If you hear no objection, just calmly reject such questions as being irrelevant to your professional work and your testimony. This will all be covered later in more detail.

Previous Writings or Testimony

Sometimes, you are hired in a case that resembles one in which you previously testified. You also may have previously published opinions on the same subject matter. Look carefully at the details of the case and the previous case or publication. Be aware, in advance, of any conflicts or inconsistencies between a position previously taken and one that you may take in this new matter.

TACTIC: To justify an opinion in a current case that differs from one expressed in a previous case, you must

explain the differences in the facts and why they lead to different opinions.

You may choose not to take the case because you simply do not want the new position to put you on the defensive, but if you do, discuss previous writings or testimony with the new possible client. You should jointly agree whether you are still the right expert for this matter.

Formalizing Your Retention as an Expert

Once an attorney decides to retain you, and you accept that retention, details of your agreement need to be put into writing. A law firm may have a standard contract they use for experts, or see Appendix E for a sample contract you may write yourself.

Time frames are important in the legal system. As soon as possible, determine any known dates for depositions, trials, and close of discovery. Lawyers know that experts have their own consulting schedules. You should determine what time constraints the lawyers have so you can work your schedule around them. Similarly, you should keep them informed of any time periods that you have already blocked out, or that become blocked out because of other commitments.

Consider the time that you will have to commit to investigations, testing, or interviews. Also bear in mind that you will often have to block out days or weeks in your schedule for various case activities such as testimony. You should anticipate frequent rescheduling or cancellations. These schedule changes can sometimes strain family plans.

It is important to consider the broader issue of malpractice, which is not limited to attorneys and is not constrained only to honesty or ethics. Experts and other witnesses are subject to laws governing perjury, which is lying under oath. In states like Pennsylvania, expert witnesses have been subject to liability for any negligence in the preparation of their materials for testimony. Be sure to obtain legal advice about adding a clause to your retainer contract that would subject malpractice disputes to arbitration.

Getting Paid for Your Work

When I first started my role of expert witness, one of my first questions was, "how much I should charge?" At the time, I was doing other consulting so I just charged the same consulting rate. As I discovered, rates for expert witnesses generally exceed standard consulting rates. If you do a quick search on Google for expert witness consulting rates, you will discover what your competition charges. Some expert witness servicing organizations also publish lists of rates, ranging from low to high, that exist for your specialty.

It bears repeating that rates do vary according to your specialty, and your experience. If you're a new expert witness, pick a rate near the lower end of the range. You can plan to increase that to the midrange after several cases, and then into the higher range after additional cases. Reassess your rates every year or two, adjusting them upwards in concert with your growing expertise and with normal inflationary pressures. Naturally, if economic conditions warrant it, you can reduce your rates.

Creating a Fee Schedule

Generally, expert witnesses charge for their time by the hour, although some experts in high-priced medical specialties charge by the day. I do not advise using a flat daily rate, independent of number of hours worked, although I do suggest a minimum daily rate for travel days. When I travel away from the office, my fee schedule specifies that I will bill my hourly rate, but with at least eight hours charged for any day that I am away from my office on my client's behalf. A minimum daily rate guarantees that you will receive payment for at least a typical eight hour workday. If the attorneys turn your day into twelve or fourteen hours, you may charge them for twelve or fourteen hour's worth of service at your hourly rate.

Whether by the day or the hour, the rates depend in part on your industry and in part on your background, credentials, and expert witness experience. A neurosurgeon might well command $1000 an hour or $10,000 a day, while another expert in a specialty that does not require the same years of academic study may only earn $100, $200 or $300 an hour.

Charging the same hourly rate for your time, regardless of the activity, values time evenly. Though testifying in court is more stressful than reading case materials in your office, those activities take time so it is logical to charge a consistent hourly rate for that time. Experts who vary their rates usually charge more for testimony time, which everyone recognizes can be stressful and challenging. So if you do charge varying rates for your time, upping the fee for testimony time will be the most palatable.

Some attorneys may ask to pay a lower rate for travel time but could be willing to pay a higher rate for testimony time. While some experts do reduce their travel rate, others do not. The ones who do not reduce for travel generally explain to the attorneys involved that they work on materials for the case while they travel. This makes the travel time argument moot, and lets you use the time efficiently.

TACTIC: You determine your rates. Some experts charge less and sometimes half the normal rate when they are traveling to and from an activity. These same experts may charge twice as much for testimony time. Most experts charge door-to-door for travel time.

I cannot say whether these variable rates produce more work for experts, but, in my experience, reducing rates for travel time does seem to be well received.

Another interesting consideration arises when a client wants you to offer a flat rate. Sometimes, you can set a fair and flat rate for a laboratory exam, or a specific scientific or medical test or procedure. It is reasonable to offer flat rates for those services. However, do not accept or offer a flat rate for general services. It is nearly impossible to ascertain in advance the number of hours you will have to spend doing research or analyses or tests or reconstructions for a case. After you begin your work on a case, it's also likely that the attorney will ask you to do additional tasks beyond those discussed in your first conversations. You should make sure that the phraseology of your retainer agreement covers your fees for any such additional work.

Asking for a Retainer

Should you ask for a retainer? Yes, you should. If a case appears simple, a modest retainer fee equivalent to two or three hours of your consulting rate may be fair. You can reduce your initial retainer fee under special circumstances or for limited scope of work. In the same fashion, you can raise your retainer at other times when the initial work will be dramatically greater. After assessing how many hours of initial work you will need to perform, let that guide you to the size of your retainer.

Be specific about the initial expectations so that you can quantify the initial retainer. Ask, and agree, on the materials you must read, the research or investigations you must complete, and consider what tests you must run. Confirm your understanding with an email, a fax or a letter, depending on the urgency of the work. Then, wait until you've received the retainer check or payment before beginning the work. If the attorney tells you that the job is urgent, send him wire transfer information so that he can wire your retainer directly to your bank account. This can easily happen in a 24-hour period.

Always ask for an initial payment before you begin work on a case or you might end up working for nothing. If, by the end of the case, the hours you spent did not consume the retainer, you should refund the difference.

Occasionally an attorney will ask you to do work for free. A free first telephone conversation represents goodwill and can be an encouragement to hire you when the case seems right. Doing analysis or research for attorneys and charging them nothing is unprofessional. On the other hand, you can certainly consider pro-bono work from time to time, just as attorneys occasionally do.

One novel element remains to consider. As your reputation grows, attorneys will sometimes retain you just to be sure that the other side cannot hire you. As a result, you should value the use of your name as an expert witness, and consider imposing a minimum fee whenever an attorney wants to retain you. You can apply this minimum charge against services, so it will have no impact on the total cost to the client unless the attorney never uses your services.

Obtaining Approval for Extra Work

Once you do begin work on a case, you should be sensitive to your total fees. Invariably, either the attorney or the client will want an estimate of the total fee you expect. Expect to prepare initial and ongoing estimates. Initial estimates will sometimes determine whether the attorney hires you or not. Ongoing estimates can put constraints on your efforts. Provide a range of dollars for any estimates. The client may hope for the lower number, but receiving an invoice that remains below your upper range will at least not shock them. Any bill that exceeds the estimate's top number will require that you obtain approval for further work since you will have gone beyond the initial expectations.

If your investigations suggest that additional tests or research should be performed, you have to convey that to the attorney and client. Generally, they have no choice but to go along with your suggestion. Sometimes, however, your attorney will decline a request for extra work. At these times, you will probably have to do without. But remember that each of your opinions has to have a solid basis. If the extra work eliminated prevents you from legitimately expressing a final opinion, you should inform your attorney and you should avoid expressing such an opinion.

TACTIC: You should receive approval from the attorney and client for extra work on your part that will exceed earlier estimates. Otherwise, you risk nonpayment and an angry client.

Asking for Advance Payments

As you can see from looking at the sample retainer contract in Appendix E, my terms require both an advance retainer and a replenishment of all or part of the retainer from time to time. The amount of replenishment depends on what additional work the attorney requires of me. Some experts require that the attorney or client maintain a minimum retainer. To do so, you should bill to restore that minimum whenever the balance in the pre-paid account for the client falls below a specific level. Ask for new advance payments whenever it becomes apparent that additional work will deplete the existing balance in the client's account.

Generally, your client will not have to replenish the retainer if the additional work only requires one to several hours. But you should request advance payment in the following instances:

1. If a sudden surge occurs in discovery materials for your review.

2. If your attorney requests that you travel for conferences and meetings.

3. If any investigations require you to travel to job sites or company offices for observations, meetings, and any other explorations.

4. If your deposition has been scheduled. You will have to reserve a variable number of days in your schedule for the deposition, for a pre-deposition conference, and possibly for the travel time as well.

5. If a trial has been scheduled; you will have the same considerations of blocking out time for possible travel, meetings, and testimony.

You should also estimate airfare, hotel, car, and food expenses as well. You can include those in requested advance payments. If you ask for advance payments, ask for them well in advance. Larger companies often have processing delays for invoices or payment requests. You do not want those delays to stand in the way of your work. Do not wait until the last minute to ask for advance payment. Your business needs to be organized enough to estimate the size of advance payments. You can base those payments on discussions with the attorney about the progress of the case and what work you anticipate will be required of you.

The most important advance payment is the one that precedes a trial. Be firm in asking for advance payment for your expected billings before traveling to testify at a trial. Clients have already spent a large sum of money by the time a trial begins. If the client loses in the trial, he either may not be able, or choose not, to pay you. But because he needs your testimony at the trial, put the pressure on him to pay beforehand and not on you to collect afterward.

TACTIC: Receiving advance payment for your trial testimony time permits you to respond "No" to the potential cross examining question of whether the client owes you any money.

If the client has already paid you, you can honestly point out that the verdict in the case will have no influence on your testimony.

Keeping Records and Submitting Invoices

As a consultant or an entrepreneur, you probably already invoice for services and do not require any help with preparing invoices to submit to clients. If you do need a new or more efficient method, QuickBooks is useful software that can manage your finances as well as prepare invoices for clients. It also keeps track of how much money individual clients owe you for legal services.

Clients frequently write checks to attorneys for their services, and payments for your invoices then come from client accounts at the law firm. In these cases, the attorney or his law firm will pay your bills when you submit them. Sometimes the clients will pay your invoices directly. Either way, however, take time to document your work and prepare invoices for submission. To keep everyone apprised of your progress, it is best to submit a copy of your invoice to both the client and the attorney. As your work progresses, keep records of what you do, the dates on which you do it, how much time you spend, who you have met, and with whom you have spoken. These records will help you to prepare your invoices.

You should always provide minimal details on an invoice, and should never include any confidential information. For example, you should not include details of private conversations. You can write that you spoke to or met with an individual, read something, or performed a series of tests. Put dates and a brief summary but no further details on the invoice. Submit your invoices regularly, based on how much work or time you spend.

Maintain a record in your file folder of your time and your expenses. Allocate one or more lines each day that you work on the case. Note the date and the hours you spent and what you did. If you have different billing rates for different activities, then keep track of those activities separately.

You should keep a log of each telephone call from the attorney about the case. When you receive a call from an attorney, note the start time of the call, the date and the end time of the call. You should include these phone conversations as part of your regular billings, but again, do not write any confidential information in your notes or on the invoice.

Additionally, keep track of any out-of-pocket expenses for which you might charge as well. This includes copying, binding, or printing. It also includes third-party services for graphics and exhibit preparation, shipping, and travel expenses for hotels, food, taxis, and rental cars.

You can take the approach that you receive such a high wage for your time as an expert that it's petty to charge for minor expenses. That is reasonable, but you will still have additional non-trivial expenses and should charge for them.

There is one final note about charging for anything, trivial or not. Once you have established yourself as an expert witness, you may occasionally be asked to offer your services for free ('pro bono' work) or for discounted fees. This usually only happens after you've established a reputation. People who cannot otherwise afford an expert witness may approach you for help, and will hope to receive your help at no charge. At other times, foundations or charitable organizations may ask you to offer your services at discounted rates because of the good works that they perform. In both cases, you have an opportunity to do a good deed at nominal cost to yourself, other than the time you might expend doing it. Let your morals and ethics, and hopefully a willingness to contribute back to the community, be your guide. As a side benefit, however, all such cases add to the overall experience that you can claim and also bring to bear on future case work.

Summary of Lesson 2

In this lesson, you learned three major issues of importance to expert witnesses. First, we covered the strongly emphasized ethical approach to your work as a witness, from investigations and meetings to testimony. Ethics must underscore your work as a witness. Second, I explained ways to arrange and document your retention by a law firm. Finally, we discussed how to price your services, bill for them, and ensure that you receive payment for your work.

3

Getting Hired by Lawyers

Lawyers have specialties, and while the largest firms can handle virtually any litigation, other firms specialize.

Where Are These Lawyers?

The first step to creating clients from lawyers is to understand where to look. The biggest firms handle the biggest cases; they have lawyers and support personnel that can work on various facets of a large case. The largest law firms employ lawyers that specialize in different kinds of litigation. Other firms offer specialized case services; they may limit themselves to financial cases, intellectual property cases, medical cases or accident cases. Solo practitioners and law firms with just a few lawyers on staff may specialize in an area such as accidents or employment law. Learn which law firms mesh best with your expertise.

For instance, some law firms specialize in automotive accidents or in insurance cases. If you are an automotive engineer, you might be hired as an expert witness in cases that involve cars, or issues that range from safety considerations to accident reconstruction. If you are an accountant, a financial or investment attorney might need your services in litigation that requires analysis or reconstruction of financial records. If your experience is in copyrights or patents, then you can expect to find your legal clients at firms that specialize in copyright or patent infringement.

Letting the Lawyers Learn About You

So how can you make sure your name and credentials get to those lawyers? Advertise in a journal or magazine that focuses on their part of the law. A small advertisement about your expert witness services that includes your website address may get the ball rolling and the phones ringing.

Do not sound overly aggressive or overly biased toward one kind of client, i.e., in favor of the plaintiff or the defense. You can easily eliminate fifty percent of your potential clientele by doing this. Worse still, if you eventually testify, an opposing attorney may use your ads against you to establish your bias toward one side or the other, which will reduce your credibility with a jury.

Although some experts regularly use print advertising, my preference is to use the Internet for free or relatively inexpensive advertising.

TACTIC: Do not use advertising that sounds aggressive or skewed toward one side or the other.

Direct contact is an effective form of marketing; it can be time consuming, but a visit to a large firm where many lawyers may need your services can be worth it. First identify law firms that specialize in the area of law that may need your expertise. Call the firm to determine which of their attorneys specializes in cases involving your expertise, and try to arrange meetings to present your credentials. If you can meet with more than one lawyer during your visit, that is even better.

Increasingly, lawyers are using the Internet to find experts. In the past, it was difficult for expert witnesses to present themselves personally online, but the video registry at www.expert-witnesses.net solves that difficulty. A database entry lists your standard credentials and the site offers an option to upload a video of you speaking and demonstrating your presentation skills. This gives attorneys the opportunity to see and hear you, an important part of your value to them.

Speaking and Writing to Attract Attention

If your specialty has its own regulatory or certifying agency, or licensing authority, you might consider speaking at conferences. Offering a relevant speech for free can have a substantial marketing effect, as well as enhance your CV.

Plan to write articles for journals or magazines that focus on your expertise. You can also write articles for lawyers about the connection between your specialty and the law. Naturally, you would write this from your perspective as an available expert consultant or witness, and not from the perspective of a lawyer.

A direct mailing to attorneys or law firms about your availability is not worth the time or money for new expert witnesses. However, after you establish yourself as an expert, it is a good idea to maintain contact with the attorneys with whom you have worked.

Lawyers move frequently, especially the ones who work with or for bigger firms. Addresses change. E-mails change. Phone numbers change. If you do not communicate with them once a year, they will forget about you. You can maintain contact easily and acceptably with a seasonal greeting card around the New Year. You can use any change of your own e-mail, phone number, or address as an excuse to send out a reminder about your existence.

As a member of an industry association, or any large professional group, you may have access to member listings in either email or postal mail form. Take advantage of those lists to put the word out to colleagues. You have legitimate access to them, and colleagues are more likely to read your communication if it is not spam or junk mail from an unknown source. I know professionals who join attorney groups as affiliate or non-attorney members because their professional specialty overlaps with the focus of the law group.

Have Your Own Website

Having a website is of paramount importance. Get one. The Internet is at the heart of nearly everything nowadays, and attorneys will turn to it at a moment's notice to seek out potential experts.

TACTIC: The name of your website is critical. Specifically, a well-chosen domain name will dramatically improve your ranking on search engines.

For example, choosing www.expertwitnesstraining.com as a domain name for expert witness training demonstrates that fact. Incorporating your specialty subject as part of the domain name will rank your site higher for its intended purpose with the search engines. A well chosen domain name provides the best visibility to lawyers looking for your expertise.

Make sure your website looks professional and reflects your background, skills, expertise, and professionalism, even if you have to hire a website designer or programmer to do it for you. Follow up regularly to enhance your website's content, and continue to market it to and through the search engines. Effective website design will do that for you. You should certainly consider hiring a consulting firm that specializes in and has years of experience in Search Engine Optimization (SEO). While artistic elements are appreciated, lawyers are more interested in your website's content. Attorneys are less concerned with your website's jazziness than your credentials, presence, and skills.

TACTIC: *Always ask potential clients how they found your name and number.*

It will help future marketing efforts to analyze the success of the different methods you used to market your services or increase your visibility. Each year, evaluate which techniques accounted for the largest number of contacts for your services. If you spend money on promotion, you should know whether it is worth spending it again in the following year or two. However, don't be disappointed if some callers do not know how they found your name or number. A common response is that they found your name somewhere on the Internet.

Marketing

So you think you're doing it all right, but the phone is not ringing? You are a specialist and you have your day job, but no lawyer has offered you a job yet as an expert consultant or witness. It won't happen without proactive effort on your part.

A Professional CV

Successful marketing requires a solid CV, which must contain a number of key elements:

- Your name and contact information.
- Your educational background. In chronological order, list universities or colleges attended, the degrees earned, and any other unique scholastic accomplishments. Include any awards earned, and in all cases, list the dates.
- Your work experience. List your jobs in reverse chronological order with your recent work experience listed first. If any gaps exist in the chronology, you should be prepared to explain why you were not working during that time period. Generally, your work history defines the roles you have played in industry or government. It should suggest growing experience, responsibility, and breadth of knowledge.

Other things may not be as obvious, but remain valuable:

- List any professional certifications, licenses, or other credentials that you hold. Even though I do not sell real estate, I did study the subject and passed the examination to receive a credential as a real estate broker. This helped me land a law case that involved computers in a real estate litigation. Including my black belt certification in jujitsu on my CV helped me land a case because the lawyers felt confident that I could calmly resist aggressive attorneys on the other side during cross examination.
- Include membership in any professional organization in your field, such as the American Medical Association. List the organization name, any special responsibilities you have in the organization, and the date on which you first joined.

- Include other professional activities such as articles or books you have written, patents you might own, or workshops and classes you have developed or taught.
- You may have skills in unrelated fields. Those skills may or may not be licensed or certified and could include special awards, community service, or government service. Do not list what you did in high school, but do not dismiss the potential value of activities you have learned as an adult.

TACTIC: The structure of your CV, especially its length, is important. An expert witness must be both precise and concise. Condense your experience into one or two pages at most. You can always provide additional details during testimony.[7]

Potential clients can always ask you for more information, and you can give more on the telephone or on the witness stand. If you want to offer other services, create a brochure that contains this additional information.

Some CVs focus on the chronology of experience or certifications. Others are organized to emphasize the logical nature of your background, with sections for industry experience, academic experience, research, and development. You'll notice in my sample CV (see Appendix F) that I use both approaches. Some attorneys look for chronology and others look for skill sets. Merging both approaches offers something of value to the general

---

[7] Some attorneys do prefer more detailed CVs, especially with medical experts. They believe that the more information that appears on a CV, the more expert their witness appears.

mix of attorneys. They may only spend five or ten seconds looking at your CV in print to decide whether to call you. Let them quickly see the key sections of interest.

My actual CV includes a second page because I have written 30 books and starred in over 25 training videos and DVDs. Books and video presentations demonstrate your ability to speak confidently in public. If you have been published, you should include a list of publications as part of a second page in your CV. Include them as well on a page of your website.

You can provide on your website a representative sample of the types of cases in which you have participated. Your sample could show the number of cases in which you have been retained, whether the plaintiffs/prosecution or the defense retained you, a brief description of each case, and the categories involved, such as computer forensics or copyright infringement. Alternatively, you can provide such a detailed list only on request.

My list of cases on my website also indicates the year of the case and the location by country or state, which helps to attract new cases that want experience in their local courts. I avoid including precise case identifiers, the law firms involved, or the parties to the case. That is just too much information, and may have confidentiality issues as well. First, I do not want those attorneys bothered without my knowledge by requests for references. Second, if a prospective new attorney is interested in one of my listed cases, he can ask me about it.

Listing You and Your Credentials

If your website appears on the first page of the Google or Yahoo search engine results, then you may not need any additional visibility. If you are not yet as busy as you'd like, I suggest alternative techniques listed in this section. Lawyers will look in several places to find experts.

- universities where you teach or do research

- membership rolls of professional or technical societies

- large companies that specialize in your discipline

- other lawyers with whom you have worked

- smaller but highly reputed consulting firms

If any of these locations maintain their own copies of your credentials or CV, make note of each location and keep your information current in their copy. Tell everyone you know about your interest in expert witness opportunities.

Apart from my own website, internet registries and intermediary organizations are two of my favorite techniques for getting expert witness jobs:

1. Your primary visibility on the web for expert witness jobs is your own website. This is essential for experts at any experience level. It is inexpensive and can readily help experienced experts to maintain a busy schedule.

2. Internet Registries can help build and maintain a work level for experts with limited to moderate experience. The cost is nominal and registries provide a valuable adjunct to your website, especially if your own website has no significant search engine visibility.

3. Intermediary organizations are an excellent choice for beginning experts with no contacts in the legal arena. These companies offer the easiest way to establish a new expert witness presence with lawyers. They can also maintain a long term job flow with no promotional efforts required on your part.

Using Internet Registries

Let's talk about those Internet registries. Some specialty companies maintain databases – registries – of experts in a variety of disciplines, like engineering, computers, medicine, and hundreds of other subjects. Registries charge you a fee to provide added visibility for your credentials on the Internet; this is a more focused search site than a standard Internet search engine.

Accessing one of the website registries produces a list of specialized experts in seconds, saving attorneys time and money. While some attorneys still do global searches on Google, many have learned that searching registries is much more productive. Having your name and credentials in one of the registries listed below will enable attorneys to find you easily.

The registries provide simple displays of your name and contact information, along with a textual listing of your principal specialties and credentials. The registries also advertise in different ways to encourage attorneys to look for expert witnesses in their registry database. The primary downside to a registry with many experts is that the attorneys may find you <u>and</u> your competitors during the same search.

Check out the registries listed below, look at their current pricing, and spend money on one or more of them to help expand your visibility on the Internet.

Internet Registries of Expert Witnesses:

almexperts.com
> Includes court reporters, as well as other consultant and litigation support services.

expertpages.com
> Established in 1995. Well worth knowing about and considering.

expert-witnesses.net

Established in 2010, this inexpensive registry allows you to augment your standard credentials with a video clip of yourself, a dramatic benefit. Attorneys will not have to wonder whether you will sound and look good on the witness stand. You can also format your own CV for distribution.

experts.martindale.com/For-Experts/List-Your-Services.html

Martindale-Hubbell's directory of expert witnesses allows a free entry. Attorneys know this company well, but it only has a bare bones expert listing and search capability. Nevertheless, their price is well worth an entry.

hgexperts.com/addex.asp?fc=yes

Well established with lawyers. Their price point seems well worth trying them out for a year or two.

jurispro.com

Extensive and valuable information for experts.

roundtablegroup.com/experts/index.cfm

The Round Table Group is one of the best and largest directories and their website contains much useful information for expert witnesses.

seakexperts.com

SEAK is a credible organization that offers a printed catalog of experts for lawyers, as well as valuable training materials for experts. They are a bit on the expensive side, but they deserve their good reputation in the industry.

witness.net

The Expert Witness Network is yet another registry offering listing services for experts, although it appears to charge attorneys for searching services.

forensisgroup.com.

The Forensis Group offers different plans that range from a simple annual listing fee to an Intermediary approach that takes a piece of the action every time you get a case. Call them to discuss your options.

Using Intermediary Organizations

Expert brokerages, called Intermediaries, will list you and your credentials in their own private database or registry, and then promote your availability to law firms.

You sign a contract, agreeing to work for a fixed rate on an hourly basis. When they find you a job, they will charge the law firm that engages you a rate that is higher than your standard consulting rate. They keep the difference.

TACTIC: Generally, Intermediaries charge you nothing up front, pay their own promotional and marketing costs, and act as your agent in obtaining litigation support jobs for you.

If you are still a relatively new expert witness, you can expect to receive your current consulting rate from these intermediaries. They will add $50-$150 per hour to your rate and charge that higher figure to the hiring law firm. The extra hourly rate beyond your normal consulting rate determines how much money they earn in total. This can add up dramatically, especially in cases that continue for months and years, with every single one of your hours contributing to their bottom line.

When they find a job for you, the good news for you is that you would otherwise never have heard of the job without them. The good news for them is that once they find you this job, they have to do little else other than collect the money from the law firm every month and pay you. They risk nothing other than their upfront time and energy to find you the law cases to work on.

Once you start receiving cases from these organizations, you will realize that attorneys are willing to pay these higher rates for your services. This signifies that you probably can raise your own consulting rates. However, as you raise your consulting rates, these intermediaries must raise their rates.

Intermediaries have to meet business criteria for profit margins. Consequently, the final rate they charge law firms may exceed what the firms are willing to pay, and you may then lose possible new cases. To avoid that, you may have to revise downward your agreed-upon consulting rates when you use an intermediary organization. On the surface this sounds not ideal, but you receive additional business and are earning more money than you were. Not a problem.

Intermediary organizations for expert witnesses:

expertresources.com

> Well established and professional company that connects experts with high level cases across the USA.

lexpertresearch.com

> Formed and run by a former attorney who promotes her ability to understand attorneys' needs when connecting them to expert witnesses.

newnexperts.com

> National Expert Witness Network specializes in intellectual property cases but takes a professional approach to any expert who contacts them.

tabexperts.com

> A family business for years, their intermediary efforts are uniquely personal and professional at the same time.

tasanet.com

> TASA is another experienced and professional company that can successfully connect experts to cases in states around the USA.

teklicon.com

> An experienced and professional expert agency with solid connections in the intellectual property legal community. They have and can find technical subject matter experts for IP attorneys around the country.

Other Approaches for Getting the Word Out

Many promotional techniques exist for expert witnesses, subject only to the time, energy, and/or money you are willing to put into advancing your expert witness career:

- Write articles. You can write articles for journals in your own specialty, for magazines or publications aimed at the general public. If your specialty area, like mine in computer forensics, might have appeal directly to lawyers, you can consider submitting articles to legal publications. You can also write articles on the Internet. A wide variety of websites publish useful articles about a myriad of subjects.

TACTIC: Social networking sites like Twitter and Facebook may appeal to you. If you use them for networking to attorneys, you should maintain complete professionalism in your posts. Silly, stupid, and sarcastic posts in these public settings will only return to haunt you later.

- <u>Speak</u> at legal conferences about your specialty.

- Become a <u>published book author</u>. Attorneys will often hunt for authors who have written entire books about the technical subject of their case. Being a published author adds credibility to your credentials when they do consider whether to hire you.

- Network with new colleagues at <u>professional meetings</u>. Many specialists and field experts do not want to be expert witnesses but may still be contacted. Tell your colleagues about your interest and willingness to be an expert witness. They may then refer you to attorneys.

- You can occasionally send a <u>focused mailing</u> to a subset of attorneys with cases in your specialty. For example, attorneys who specialize in automotive accidents might like to know that as an automotive design engineer you are interested in expert witness work. In a mailing like this, a simple cover letter with your CV/brochure will be enough for attorneys to file your materials for later reference.

- <u>Print advertising</u> is another option. This could include advertising in your local Yellow Pages, especially if your specialty is also localized, like local real estate or building appraisals. You might consider advertising in specialty legal publications, although these can be costly.

What Do Lawyers Consider When Hunting for Experts?

Knowing what lawyers think and consider can guide your efforts at getting them to notice you. Some things are more obvious than others. For example, if an attorney has a high profile murder case or a $100 million civil liability case, he probably wants an expert with an established reputation, testimonial experience, impeccable credentials, a good number of years in the specialty, and quite possibly a PhD. Because litigation experience is such a big priority, attorneys ask other attorneys for recommended expert witnesses.

Some of the subtler considerations made by lawyers will be reflected in the choice between an academic and a hands-on expert. For example, in a civil suit involving the failure of a blood infusion pump in a hospital's coronary care unit, a hands-on engineer who regularly repairs such devices at the hospital may be more valuable to the case than a PhD in biomedical engineering who designs them. The repair engineer can speak to failure rates, rates of service, and the hands-on issues involved in a hospital. An academically trained bioengineering device designer might be less useful to the particular case because his or her expertise is in rates of flow in the pump, not failure rates.

What does this mean for you? If you have hands on industry experience, your marketing strategy should emphasize the benefit you can bring to cases that rely on applied knowledge and expertise. If you have substantial academic experience, emphasize your book-knowledge and teaching skills for cases relying on theory or design.

Lawyers prefer experts who are resistant to Daubert challenges. Based on the Supreme Court ruling in the Daubert case, this could be you if:

- You or the methodologies used in your work have been published in peer reviewed publications.

- Your peers accept your methodologies.

- You are meticulous in your approach to ascertaining and considering a wide range of possibilities.

- Your approach to data analysis is extremely thorough; this will satisfy the lawyer who realizes that courts look toward both qualitative and quantitative adequacy of information in expert investigations.

I'll expand further on Daubert fundamentals and requirements in later lessons on expert reports, depositions, and trial testimony. Your appreciation of Daubert principles and your ability to apply them will help lawyers decide that you are the expert for them.

Beyond all the technical and professional knowledge you may have, you must also be personable. Over the course of a case, your retaining attorney will spend time with you on the telephone, meeting with you in conferences, working with you on affidavits or declarations or reports, and on preparing you for testimony. If you are a bore, and the attorney can't enjoy a meal with you, he will likely hire another, more personable expert. So put your best foot forward when you do meet attorneys for possible expert witness work.

TACTIC: Attorneys interpret sociability and likeability at your first meeting as a big plus for a hiring decision. As a first consideration, an attorney thinks about the impression you may have on jurors.

Convincing Attorneys That You Can Help Them

The introductory phone call is your biggest opportunity to influence an attorney's decision to hire you. Show him that you already understand litigation support and that you know your specialty. You can begin by suggesting how you would approach a case he has. Be proactive with your knowledge and skills.

Once you have a little experience under your belt, you can offer free technical advice with regard to a case, or even share things that other attorneys have done in similar cases. You are not giving advice to a lawyer on the law, but you are sharing your experiences in other cases that are similar. If you have more experience in a particular kind of case than the attorney has then your experience may help him to identify areas of need. You could suggest the steps you might take to reach an opinion in the case. This approach uses your specialty expertise as a selling tool in a low-key way.

Appearance and Demeanor

Do your credentials and experience support your claim to being an expert, and does your CV instantly convey that claim? Do you sound good when you speak, and do you speak well and clearly? Shyness does not become an expert witness. Good eye contact is a valued skill.

Can you dress well? Think of your initial meeting with an attorney as a job interview. Wear business clothing. If you see that the atmosphere in the office is more casual, then you might dress down a bit for future meetings but never dress more casually than those you will be working with. You want to impress attorneys with your professionalism, and your appearance contributes to that. When you attend a deposition or a trial, you should take the same approach to appearance as well. You want everyone to see you as both serious and professional in appearance as well as in demeanor.

TACTIC: Sloppiness in your appearance suggests carelessness in your work.

You should consider one more thing. Do not overdress by wearing flashy clothes or flashy jewelry. One lawyer I worked for pointed out to me that the opposing expert had on a $10,000 Rolex watch during a deposition. He said jurors don't want it rubbed in their noses exactly how much money experts make. The attorney planned to make a point of the watch with the jurors if given the opportunity.

Growing Your Role with Each Case

Once hired, you can immediately contribute to the process by helping attorneys understand the technical facts. In addition, you can help by formulating a series of technical questions that your retaining attorney can use when he writes various legal documents. Know what relevant questions you can ask. You are the one who will be able to explain the technical responses to the attorney. It is part of your role to guide the attorney in the discovery process. Help construct the technical questions that will require technical answers from the other side. This should help to uncover the technical facts of the case that you then use to formulate your eventual opinion(s).

It is part of your role to help attorneys understand information received from the other side. You will quickly learn that in many cases your retaining attorneys do not know what questions to ask. You will have an incredible advantage over your competition if you understand in advance how to help your clients articulate their needs.

TACTIC: Lawyers need you to help formulate questions to ask and explain the answers they receive. What the attorneys call "interrogatories" are questions that they submit to the other side in the case. These questions

*lead to answers, and help them in the discovery phase
of the case.*[8]

Once you understand the technical portions of the case,
you can suggest interrogatories that will help to uncover the
technical facts for both your attorney and you.

Sometimes, you'll help your attorney determine the most
and least important technical elements of the case. Your role will
also include helping the attorneys decide what questions to ask
the opposing experts during a deposition or in a trial. If you
accompany your attorney to the deposition of an opposing expert,
you can help enormously by identifying initial questions to ask, as
well as follow-on questions.

Remember though, you should not design your questions
as an advocate for your side. You want the technical facts, and
your attorney needs to know the quantity and quality of technical
information the other side's expert possesses. You may agree or
disagree with the side that hired you, but you must maintain a
level of objectivity. It is your job to obtain new facts, analyze
others, and explain the key facts that form the basis of your
eventual opinions.

To grow as an expert witness, and contribute more
successfully with each case, you should understand the legal
process. Specifically, you must understand what is needed by an

---

[8] Actual interrogatories are used in most states, but not all, and in federal courts.
Even if formal interrogatories are not required in your case, your ability to
formulate questions for the technical experts of the other side will nevertheless
be invaluable.

attorney from you as a technical expert. It is not a question of whether you have the technical expertise; the question is whether you can apply your expertise and knowledge of the subject matter to the elements of the case. Can you organize your information well, present it effectively to your clients, and testify to it successfully in a court of law? You have to understand how the legal process works to help attorneys organize and present their case, at least to the extent the case relies on your expertise. Each new case offers you a new learning opportunity to help the next retaining attorney even more by understanding both their role and your own.

Conflicts

A quick note about conflicts. The first question an attorney may ask you is whether you have any conflicts in the case. That doesn't mean "are you conflicted about the issue in the case?" It could mean: do you have any other work with anybody involved in the case? For instance, are you currently working on another matter for any of the attorneys in this matter, on either side? Are you working on another job with a law firm that is working on this case? Are you related to, or friends with, anybody involved in the case? Is there any connection between this matter and anybody in your personal life? You must think of all possibilities. If it comes out later that a conflict existed, everything you do may become useless and the court may not permit you to deliver testimony as an expert in the matter. Recognize and accept conflicts when they exist; you have to pass on such a case and just wait for the next one.

Summary of Lesson 3

Getting hired by attorneys requires that you understand which kinds of lawyers look for experts with your credentials. Knowing where they look and what they think about when they look will help you to become more visible to them.

Be sure to have a well designed website. Augmenting that visibility with additional positioning on Internet registries and with intermediary organizations will be money well spent in building your presence in legal circles.

4

Working with Attorneys

These lessons concentrate on your role as an expert, both from your perspective and from the perspective of the lawyer or client who hires you. If you only consider your job from one perspective, you will be like a martial artist who learns only how to punch or kick, but not to block and defend. From the other side's perspective, you are the opposing expert.

It is imperative to consider both points of view. The ways in which you help your retaining attorney will change according to whether the plaintiff or the defense retains you.

As an expert, regardless of whether you work for the plaintiff or the defendant, your key role is to educate your attorney-client in any technical elements of the case. This includes known technical facts in the case, plus newly discovered information of a technical nature. These ongoing discoveries may come from your research, additional documentation from the other side, or just miscellaneous discovery during your investigation. Your attorney will often ask you to help by reading and analyzing information submitted from the other expert.

Expert Witness for the Plaintiff

The expert working for the plaintiff has to do appropriate research, analysis, or investigations that lead to believable findings and defensible opinions. Early in the case, your attorney may ask you to report your preliminary observations or findings verbally. He may also ask you to write a simple declaration or affidavit addressing a limited technical portion of the case. Only after you have completed your investigation and analyses might he ask you to write the expert report that contains your complete findings.

If your attorney asks you for your opinions early in the case, you should state clearly that opinions expressed orally at this point are preliminary. Do not hesitate to say that you have not completed your investigation or analyses. You do not want to mislead your attorney, but you also do not want to lock yourself into a position that you haven't yet firmly taken, and then end up having to defend that position to your own attorney or his client.

If you are the plaintiff's expert, the opinions in your expert report are central to your work. The attorney for the plaintiff wants to offer them to support his case. First, do not stretch the truth. Do not offer an opinion or conclusion that you cannot back up completely by your research and analysis. Do not permit your attorney to pressure you into expressing an opinion that you do not fully believe and cannot fully defend by what you know as an expert. The investigative procedures and analyses that you include in your expert report should stand as a foundation for the stated opinions. You should be careful not to let your phraseology make your opinion harder to defend. For example, do not claim in your report that something is always true or is never true, even if you do not currently recognize any possible exceptions.

TACTIC: Never say 'never' and always avoid 'always' in your opinions.

Expert Witness for the Defense

The expert for the defense has the task of reading the plaintiff's expert's findings, reports, affidavits, or declarations. Your goal should be to look for factual errors, oversights, or mistaken assumptions by the other expert. Your job is to assess whether or not the other expert's research, study, procedures, or references fully support the opinions he or she expressed. Your lawyer / client will use your assessment of the other expert in case planning and possibly future questioning. What's the goal? The defense counsel generally looks for information that can be used to discredit the plaintiff's expert, casting doubt on the expert's facts or methodologies. If possible the jackpot would be to negate all of the other expert's conclusions through your study and analysis.

The defendant's expert must look at every opinion expressed in the plaintiff's expert's report. First, see if each opinion makes sense to you as an expert in this field. If it does make sense, that's fine. You can go further and verify whether the plaintiff's expert has adequately explained the procedures or science that led to his opinion. If you can find any weakness in logic, even though technically correct conclusions have been drawn, point them out to your attorney.

Further, you will probably want to point out those logical weaknesses in your own rebuttal report, which you will prepare as a direct response to the plaintiff's expert's report. Perhaps an opinion in the expert's report strikes you as incorrect or weak. Explain to your attorney why you believe this, and include it in your own rebuttal report. Whatever you write in your rebuttal report will become the subject of your own testimony for the defense.

Looking at It from the Other Side's Perspective

If you take cases for both plaintiffs and defense, then you must understand both perspectives so you can perform your role well for either side. It will help, as well, if you can anticipate what the other side's expert is likely to do. You know he or she is going to look closely at your report, so you have to be doubly careful about what you write. Think about the basis for each opinion you will express.

Regardless of whether you are acting as an expert witness for the plaintiff or for the defense, your goal is to assess whether each of the steps taken by the other side's expert made sense. Was it correct, appropriate, and complete enough to lead to the stated opinion? Assess whether any portion of the expert's logic suffered from mistaken assumption or oversight. If so, your attorney can then legitimately use your assessments to undermine the credibility of the expert or the opinion.

More than one possibility often exists. A common error made by people in general is to take the easy way out and say: "that was the only way possible." Bridge players may say there was no other way to play the cards. Backgammon players may say there was no other way to play the dice. Expert witnesses may say that their conclusion is the only sensible one. Don't assume that the way taken is the only way; look for other possibilities, and explore them.

TACTIC: If you are the plaintiff's expert, consider all the possibilities. Prepare to explain why you may have chosen one or only a subset of the possibilities as the basis for your opinion.

TACTIC: If you are the defendant's expert, list other possibilities that the plaintiff's expert should have considered, and why.

Pointing out other possibilities may be enough to generate reasonable doubt or to undermine the credibility of the other side's expert.

Assisting Attorneys during the Discovery Process

An expert witness can help during the entire process of case preparation. Naturally, you have to expertly conduct your own investigations, write your own report, and testify on your own. However, you and your technical expertise can contribute in other ways to the success of your side's efforts in the matter.

Lawyers will often submit pleadings – legal arguments – to the court. They will often ask you to write and contribute technical paragraphs of text to each pleading and then you may be asked to sign the document, called an affidavit or a declaration.

Attorneys will often prepare, as a part of the discovery process, a series of written requests called interrogatories. Attorneys on both sides of the case will submit a series of such requests for the production of information and documents. This set of formal requests is a tedious series of inquiries used to learn as much as possible about what the other side knows. Your attorneys will ask you to examine such interrogatories from the other side, and you will help them prepare such interrogatories for your side.

Review your attorney's discovery request prior to submission to ensure that the request has covered the technical elements. Ensure that the request spans all of the possible information for which he can ask, and that the phraseology of the request is technically precise. The burden in the legal system is that each side must do its best to discover relevant information from the other side. Although the discovery process permits each side to ask for documents and relevant material, the discovery requests must ask explicitly. If the document doesn't ask precisely for technical elements, the other side doesn't have to provide the information. Your job in this early phase is to ensure that documents prepared by your lawyer are both correct and complete, from a technical perspective.

Conducting an Investigation

Conducting an investigation into the details of the case demands attention to detail, planning, and care in the steps you take. As the expert in your field, determine what you need to have and what you need to do before you can draw any conclusions. You have to identify the information you need to know before forming any opinion in the case. For instance, you must assess:

- what you need to find out

- what you need to test

- what you need to reconstruct

- what mathematical equations you need to formulate

- who you need to interview

- what documents you need to read

- what software you need to use

- what information you need to compare

Words like 'painstaking,' 'methodical,' 'meticulous,' 'step-by-step,' and 'careful' should describe your approach. Generally, begin with having simple, factual discussions with your attorney, and subsequently, your attorney's client. These discussions may lead to documents either already filed or already collected by the attorney.

Your discussions with the attorney's client may lead to finding or receiving additional documents to read, or to additional persons with whom to speak. As you understand details of the case, you will collect additional information. Some of it may have already been filed as part of the case, and some of it may be accessible to the persons with whom you meet and speak. At times, you will visit the site involved or make observations of equivalent machinery or systems at another site.

Deciding What Information to Consider

You must decide what information to consider and what information to ignore.

Federal Rule of Evidence 703 demands that the basis for expert testimony must be information that is "reasonably relied on by experts in the particular field in forming opinions or inferences." The attorneys in your case are not experts in your field so, by definition, they are not competent to expertly evaluate the evidence to decide what parts of it may or may not be relevant to your opinions. Attorneys will sometimes show you only a subset of the technical information in a case. When they do that, they undermine their own case and they undercut your likelihood of success during testimony.

Make sure to ask for all relevant information, regardless of whether others might call your request irrelevant. Obvious technical information that bears on the case is relevant. So are any documents that discuss technical information, regardless of who wrote the documents. As your understanding of the case progresses, you may expand the scope of your information requests. This may come about as you learn more about various events and participants, or it may come about after reviewing other discovery materials.

In a complicated case, many boxes of evidence may exist for review, often stored at the attorney's office. Sometimes the boxes are labeled, and sometimes an index exists that clarifies what documents and materials are available. You should always look through the index or the boxes to decide what material to review in detail and what to reject before proceeding with opinion formulation. The room where the attorneys store these boxes of evidence is colloquially referred to as the war room.

Asking your attorney and client for additional details and information can save you the time or cost of finding it. If you cannot obtain what you need directly from your client or attorney, you should look further and continue your research and investigation with other sources.

TACTIC: Your testimony is stronger if you can honestly say that you personally assessed the total available information and determined what was relevant and what was irrelevant.

Using Support Staff for Data Collection or Research

At times, you may want to use associates, students, or employees to assist you in the collection or analysis of information. Your attorney may offer the use of paralegals or other employees but using your own personnel will enable you to oversee what they do, and testify about the reliability of their work. This bears on yet another Daubert-related consideration. Using your own personnel enables you to legitimately testify to your assistant's work as being routinely relied on in your particular field.

Collecting Information

Be as organized in your collection of information as you are meticulous in your study of it. Always attend meetings with a notebook, pen, clip board, recorder, and/or camera. Consider bringing miscellaneous other equipment that may be useful, depending on your discipline, such as magnifying glasses, flashlights, binoculars, and testing devices. Use these items to help make records of people, machines, context, and whatever else is pertinent to your opinions in this matter.

TACTIC: Do not rely solely on your memory of interviews or site visits.

Refer to documents by identification number and date; refer to people you meet and interview by name and date. Documenting your interviews and site visits will bolster your own memory. First, an opinion requires reference to facts, measurements, or other data to be acceptable. During testimony, you must precisely identify the details of how and when you acquired information: dates, locations, names, or simply procedures followed. Document what you saw, heard, or discovered. Second, those notes and observations can jog your memory during subsequent analysis and study, and they may also guide you to further discovery and further explorations.

Make sure to ask those you interview the correct spelling of their names, and leave your business card with them. This may result in additional information. They may not have had access to information at the time you met with them, or they may remember important information that they did not think of when you were there.

In essence, you must be able to explain and defend the steps you took to reach your opinion. Your expert report will include details of what you did, how you did it, and when.

Organizing Your Research Efforts

The goal of your research and analyses is to logically collect information relevant to the case. As you progress in this collection of relevant data, a picture will form. You will see what information relates to a particular scenario or element of the case, and how to group the materials you collect, or the results of tests you run.

If you like to organize information in files, then do so. Organize notes, documents or the materials you collect into those files. Each of those groupings may lead to a single opinion that you include in your eventual report and testimony. You can then refer to the documents as you write and build the foundation for each opinion. Finalizing opinions becomes easier if you have organized your materials such that you can readily find the information that supports each opinion.

Keeping the Attorney up to Date on Your Efforts

Whatever you record in writing or electronic form becomes discoverable by the other side in the case. This includes any emails you may write to the attorney. Think twice about putting information into email just because it's convenient or because you cannot reach the attorney on the telephone. Think twice about documentation of your interim analyses, progress, or considerations. These written materials are potential evidence and you may have difficulty recalling why you even wrote them. Worse still, they may prove embarrassing if they suggest conflicts with your final opinions.

TACTIC: Use the telephone, and not email, to keep your attorney up to date on your work!

Do not consider deleting those e-mails or throwing away documented notes in your file. Once they're written, by law you cannot blatantly destroy potential evidence. Laws concerning spoliation and obstruction of justice will govern your removal of written material from your file. This also includes misguided e-mails that your own attorney may send you with revelations about the case, or about the attorney's tactics and strategies regarding the case.

Relating to the Clients

Individuals who need lawyers are generally the named litigants in the case. They hire the attorneys, and the attorneys generally hire you as an expert witness. The client is the one who pays both you and the attorneys, so even though the lawyer or law firm may formally hire you, it's a moot point since the litigant is paying for both of you.

Stay Neutral

When you meet with clients, those who work with them, or with witnesses, they may have strong opinions about what or who was right or wrong. Just listen, ask appropriate questions, and take notes that are factual but not opinionated. Do not reveal your thinking, but only say that you are gathering facts with which to formulate opinions.

From time to time, you will determine that your client is in the wrong, that he may be "the bad guy." You must remain calm and neutral; yet, you have to share it with your attorney as soon as possible. Let the attorney decide what to do with that information. At times, the attorneys may choose to release you from the case because your opinions may no longer be able to help them. At other times, this may strongly guide the attorney into a different tack in the matter.

I have been involved in cases where my research proved that my attorney's client was in the wrong. In those cases, the research helped the attorney settle the case on better terms in civil matters, and plead the case to less burdensome terms in criminal matters. Even though you bring objectivity to your job as an expert witness, it can still be stressful when you cannot help to prove the innocence of your own client, or the guilt of the opposing party's client. However, if you have done your job properly, you can still be proud of the professional way in which you performed your investigations and your analyses. In effect, you have helped both the attorney and the client. Regardless of whether your side is in the right or in the wrong, your work efforts can help assist your attorney to obtain a better final result.

Don't be an Attorney's Hired Gun

At other times, you might need to or choose to withdraw from the case. This is especially relevant if the attorney requests that you deliver a dishonest opinion. If your attorney wants an opinion that you have not yet reached, you should clarify that it is not ethical and emphasize that you will not do that. At this juncture, you could offer to continue working, with the understanding that you will only deliver your honest opinion after you review the evidence and complete your investigation. If you are willing to use your reputation and your knowledge to give an opinion that you know is unfounded, untrue, or not researched thoroughly by you, you are gambling that the other side will not discover this. But remember, during cross examination, nearly any attorney can make a poorly prepared or dishonest expert witness sound like a fraud or an idiot.

While not the norm, some attorneys will only hire you if you agree to deliver the opinion they want. You should not accept a job from any attorney who has that expectation.

Possible Conflicts with the Attorney's Client

Because the clients ultimately pay the bills, they are more sensitive to your expenses than the attorneys. Clients know they need an attorney; they do not always understand why the attorney has to hire an expert. Worse, they do not always understand why experts are so expensive.

Since they pay the bills, many clients participate in phone conversations or meetings you have with attorneys, and sometimes they will call you directly. The best advice is to say as little as possible to the client, especially if the attorney is not present. Your job does not require that you develop a personal relationship with the client; it only requires that you receive necessary client information and materials to formulate your opinions.

Conflicts can arise if the client is anxious for the case to end, to receive your opinions, to learn what you have discovered, and to minimize your bills. The best advice is to spend as little time as possible alone with the clients. While it is inevitable that you will need to spend time in discussions with clients, try to do so with the attorney present, if possible.

Don't be a Client's Hired Gun

Clients do not always understand your objective role. Sometimes, they believe that you have been hired to espouse their position and they may try to pressure you. The easiest defense is simply to state that you are still gathering information and still working on your final opinion. Even so, clients may restate their positions, beliefs, and hopes. You should be polite, listen, but avoid any agreement.

Some clients are more subtle than others. They will not explicitly tell you what opinion they want you to express. They may simply barrage you with their views of how things happened, or what things went wrong, or why things worked as they did or did not. They may express their own opinions about events or personnel or activities, and they will tell you their version of those events. And they hope to influence your opinion.

Stay away from any suggestions of selling your opinions. In court, hired guns are not as likely to have done the research and thereby have the details to defend their opinions effectively. Word gets out about which experts, even if credentialed and knowledgeable, will sell their opinion just for their consulting fees. The term "hired gun" is demeaning, and often characterizes an expert as disreputable.

Helping Your Attorney during a Deposition

When you understand the legal elements of a case and the attorney's goals, you can help write a useful set of technical questions that can be used to ask the other expert during a deposition.

TACTIC: Writing a well phrased and precise series of questions will help your attorney put the other expert on the spot. This will enable your attorney to solicit the best possible scope of information from the other expert's responses.

Generally, attorneys do not possess the expertise to ask follow-on technical questions if they receive a rambling response. They might not understand the answer, and not know what to ask next, and your job is to explain, in English, the gobbledygook. If the other expert has made an error, you can alert your attorney. If the other expert has made an omission, your attorney can ask him to fill in the gap. If the other expert shows a lack of knowledge, your attorney can make that obvious with follow-on questions. Finally, your attorney will often need to ask additional questions beyond his initial set. When this happens, your help may be needed to phrase those additional questions precisely. Helping the attorney to phrase technical questions better will make the follow-on questioning more effective.

Sometimes, your attorney will not want to wait until a break to receive this feedback. You may be asked to pass a note if you think of relevant follow-on questions. This approach helps to draw complete responses from other experts. Some believe that playing this role casts you in the role of an advocate rather than an objective aide to the process. I disagree. You are helping the attorney discover fully what the other expert knows or does not know. The attorney decides how to use this newly discovered knowledge.

Problems Working with Attorneys

This lesson focuses on ways to work with attorneys and how the process can work to both your benefits. However, problems can arise that are nobody's fault but simply a reflection of the system and the burdens of job responsibilities.

Problems you may have with your own attorney differ from those you may have with opposing counsel. Your attorney may not have as much time to work with you as you would like. Initially, attorneys want to bring you up to speed on the case so that you can independently perform your expert witness role, and so will spend a lot of time to ensure that happens. However, if you seem competent, your attorney may just leave you to your own devices. Consequently, you may find yourself without help as you prepare the expert report or get ready for your deposition or trial testimony.

On the other hand, it can sometimes be frustrating to work with your retaining attorney. Often, you must explain the technical aspects of your work and if you do this at his office, there may be frequent interruptions. Sometimes the attorney simply does not listen, or cannot concentrate on what you have to say.

Attorneys have timelines and sometimes limits on money to spend on expert witnesses. This can explain why you will sometimes have less time than you might like.

You may decide to take a case a week before it goes to trial. Not infrequently, the opposing counsel's expert witness has already spent months reviewing evidence, making tests, coming to opinions, and even writing a report. You may not have time to do what is needed to reach well-founded opinions, and your retaining attorney may be hoping you will fall in line with his views.

TACTIC: Attorneys want your report and your testimony to be organized, clear, logical, and well presented. You will wish that they managed their own time that way.

There will be times when you should consider no longer working with the attorney who hired you. Each expert will have his or her own lines over which they will not step.

Maintaining Contact with the Attorney

Initially it is easy to maintain contact with your retaining attorney. You will see each other on scheduled dates for reports, depositions, and possibly a trial. But in the middle stages, many months or even years can pass with no visible progress in the case.

Plan to call the attorney every three months to check on the status of the case. Occasionally you will discover during such a call that the case settled and, 'oops, we're sorry we didn't let you know.' At that point, you can prepare your final bill, or prepare a refund for any remaining and unused retainer dollars.

When a case ends, thank the attorney for having hired you. This could be a simple telephone thank-you, or you could write a follow-up letter formally thanking the attorney. Even if the case did not end well for the attorney and his client, you can still leave the attorney with a good recollection of your participation in it.

TACTIC: Stay in touch with your attorney clients. Keep your contact information current.

Create and maintain a current database of your attorney clients: their complete and correctly spelled name, firm, address phone numbers, and e-mail address. Update the database often; attorneys change firms, especially the ones that work for large law firms. The post office or their employer can let you know how to reach them if they've moved.

If you move or change your phone number or e-mail address, contact the attorneys with whom you have worked and let them know. In part, that helps to keep their database of expert witness names current, and helps remind them about you.

It is a good idea to contact each attorney once a year. Send a Season's Greetings card at the end of the calendar year. Receiving such cards from business associates is common, and you will probably receive some from attorneys each year. Attorneys who send me cards are among the first I think of when asked for referrals. You can expect the same in reverse.

Summary of Lesson 4

Your expert witness role will vary somewhat depending on whether the plaintiff or the defendant has hired you. However, legal mechanics will not change, such as assisting with pleadings and interrogatories. Your work with attorneys in helping them during discovery and depositions will not change dramatically on either side of the case. Neither will your experiences with clients. In this lesson, we also discussed problems that can arise with both attorneys and their clients. I also emphasized the importance of ongoing contact with them both during the case and after the case ends.

5

Conducting an

Expert Investigation

Expert investigations can vary dramatically in content and scope. An automotive accident investigator may have to spend time at an accident site taking photographs, and follow up with interviews. A psychiatrist may conduct interviews but without having to leave her office. A computer specialist may have to make copies of hard drives and correlate the information found on those drives with the details of a crime.

What these various expert witness roles have in common is the mountains of documents to review about the case. The lawyer hiring you will usually begin with a brief synopsis, followed by some documents to read and possibly a summary. While this all could be helpful, it may represent only part of the total discovery data. Moreover, the summaries may contain oversimplifications or even errors.

TACTIC: Do not rely on attorney summaries of documentation. You must review documents of importance and relevance to draw conclusions and form opinions based on their contents.

Your responsibility, as you ramp up your investigation, is to decide which documents and evidence to review directly. Ask for any indexes that will help you sort through the contents of the war room; go to the war room and decide which documents to review. If it looks like a war zone, it could be that neither labels nor indexes exist. In this case, wade through the documents to make decisions about them, and when you use them, keep printed records of the documents by both name and date stamp identifications.

You cannot simply use a lifetime of experience in your field of expertise as justification for an expert opinion. Such an opinion, without appropriate foundation, is called a net opinion and is not strong enough for an expert witness. Your total research and analysis, and the thoroughness and carefulness with which you perform that work, is what will make your opinions legally acceptable to the judge and the jurors.

Laying the Foundation for Your Opinions

Rule 703 of the Federal Rules of Evidence spells out three classes of data or facts that an expert can consider and on which he can base his opinions:

A. Things you learn or see directly, before the trial.

B. Things you learn or see directly, at the trial.

C. Other data or facts that you hear about or learn about, as long as they are normally relied on by experts in your particular field.

The first, "Things you learn or see before the trial" can cover what you read, any discussions you have with people at accident sites, in hospitals, at job sites, or even with technical people who wrote software or who ran machinery. It can also include the results of well-defined research you've done that is relevant to the subject of the case. These activities generally happen well before the trial. The rest of this lesson focuses on what you may do, and how you may collect this evidence and information.

Regarding the second part of Rule 703, you will occasionally learn something new at the trial. Sometimes, other witnesses may introduce evidence on the witness stand for the first time. Some states require that you hear such evidence directly, which means that you might have to sit in the trial for hours or days before your testimony, listening to others testify.

The third part of Rule 703 has to do with facts that are "normally relied on by experts in your particular field." If experts in your field reasonably rely on outside labs, investigators, or assistants, then you can use information they gather as part of the basis for your opinions.

Ensuring Admissibility of Your Work

Playing by the rules of this legal game will help ensure the admissibility of your work. The goal is to convince people that your opinions are sound. Your investigations and overall work will help you to do just that. After you collect, review and study all the information about the technical elements of a case, perform the necessary tests, and follow necessary methodologies, you can form opinions that you can express in an expert report or in testimony.

TACTIC: What you do will help you technically and professionally come to the best opinions. How you do it will help ensure that your opinions are seen as 'admissible' and that they will be allowed to be heard in court.

Remember, you are on a playing field called 'the law.' You have to play by the rules in this game:

1. You must be familiar with the facts in the case and the sequence of any events that happened.

2. You must carefully document tests run, observations made, and measurements taken. Include all results, whether positive or negative.

3. Any demonstrations you plan to use during testimony have to be substantially the same as the events in the case.

4. Any materials you use in tests must be the same as were involved in the case.

5. You must document all steps followed and methods used. Use industry literature and publications to show that the chosen tests or methods are recognized as authoritative in your field.

6. Consider with your attorney whether to use and pay for an independent peer review of your analyses and work.

You very well might do solid investigative and preparatory work, but you are not an attorney so you will not know about all the legal elements of the lawyer's case. Sometimes you have to meet legal standards that vary from jurisdiction to jurisdiction; explicitly ask your attorney about the standards for your particular jurisdiction so you can choose the tests you run. For example,

Maryland, Rhode Island, or California may use different legal tests for insanity. As a psychologist, perhaps, you need that information so you can pose the right questions.

Admissibility: Forewarned is Forearmed

Lawyers will use numerous tactics to raise objections about the validity and admissibility of you, your evidence, and your opinions. Anticipate the following possibilities:

- You are not qualified by knowledge, skill, experience, training, or education in the scientific field needed for this case. In advance, prepare your explanation of why your background does indeed qualify you to offer opinions about the facts in this matter.

- Your opinions did not flow from reliable facts or data. Again, be ready to show that the facts were reliable and that your opinions did reasonably flow from them.

- You did not use reliable methods in your work. Prepare to cite examples from your field and its literature that show that you did.

- You did not run enough tests or collect enough data to justify your conclusions quantitatively. Keep accurate notes and be prepared to show that you ran the tests and collected the data needed.

- You haven't used qualitatively relevant conclusions. Make sure the facts you rely on, and the opinions you offer, are directly relevant to the case.

- You relied on hearsay to form your opinions. Ensure that any information you use, whatever the source, is routinely relied on by experts in your field.

Conversations and Meetings

In simple terms, the expert investigation and analysis begins with your first conversation with an attorney or a client. More often than not, this first contact will be from the attorney but sometimes the client makes the call in order to be sure you truly understand the relevant technical matter.

Early contact like this, as well as ongoing contacts with the client, can lead to interesting problems. During preliminary conversations, the client may reveal confidential company information or information about the case you should not have. Other times, information is revealed a month or a year later. In either case, the problem can be avoided if you make sure the attorney is present so the conversation will remain privileged.

TACTIC: You should not chat with the client about the case without the attorney present. In that event, the conversation is privileged and you will not have to reveal its contents to the other side.

Opposing attorneys are allowed to ask you questions about the content of any conversations you have had with the client alone. The revelations that come from that testimony are not always desirable. The same is true for the occasional conversation you may have with persons working for the other side – maybe a chat with another expert, a client, or a researcher during a meeting. Talking to no one but your attorney is best, especially if the other expert is a fellow professional with whom you are familiar, or a friend. The less you say to anyone on the other side, the better.

Conducting Interviews

An interview can happen spontaneously or as a planned part of your investigation. You may be on the premises of your client's company or where the event you are researching took place. You may be at a factory trying to understand an entire system in operation. Many times you will meet people who were present on the day of the event in question, and they may have valuable information.

Use open ended questions when you chat with people in spontaneous interviews. Ask them simply what they can tell you about how the system works, or how employees do their work. You can ask people what they do, how the company works, how their department works, or how the machinery and systems work. These open ended questions invite people to tell you what they know, which constitutes much of what you need to learn.

Remember: you are seeking the truth during your interviews but you may not easily discover that truth when asking questions. People will not remember information, or will remember incorrectly. You are the expert; you have to decide how to piece the facts together as you obtain them. You should always be cordial to the people with whom you speak or interview. If it's unpleasant speaking with you, they may duck out of interviews quickly.

Depending on the expertise you bring to the table, you may research events, people, equipment, software, and procedures – anything relevant to the matter. It will help if you can blend in, so wearing a suit that works for a deposition may be inappropriate when doing field research. That same suit may put off the people working in jeans or overalls. Just dress appropriately for the people you will likely meet.

You are also not there to chat about yesterday's baseball game, football game or the weather. Light banter may be okay, but don't spend time trying to become friends. You are researching a case and soliciting information. Act professionally. If you are less chatty, then the people with whom you speak will be chattier. You will have allowed them more time to give you more information.

Often these people with whom you speak want to know about the case and will ask you what you think. No matter how casually they pose the question, they are still hoping to learn your opinion. Never give that opinion to anyone other than your attorney, and do not offer it to your attorney until you have completed your research. While gathering information, you should have no opinion. Politely reply to any inquiry that you are just conducting research and gathering facts. In reality, you will only deliver this opinion to your attorney.

Conducting Site Inspections

Your site inspection may not involve talking with participants or meeting people at the site. For example, you may be analyzing the site of an automotive accident. If your expert analysis requires a personal inspection, you should observe and note as many elements of the scene as possible. Consider other factors that may have been in play on the day of the event you are researching, such as the weather, the time of day, or the lighting. Try to visit the site as close as possible to the time of day when the accident took place. Digital photographs should be identified and dated.

Date any notes that you take during your site inspection. If you oversee the handling or removal of any evidence at the site, carefully document your handling of that evidence.

Sometimes, your attorney will have to ask the opposing counsel for permission for a site inspection. In those cases, the opposing party's expert and even law enforcement personnel may attend your inspection to oversee your work. Avoid conversations with any of them regarding the investigative steps you take. Generally, you should arrange that your attorney attends as well to shield you from any of these other people in attendance.

Your site inspection may involve using or observing equipment such as computers or other operational machines. Take careful notes and include the serial numbers of the devices, or other information that will specify exactly which machinery or equipment you observed, tested, or used. You can also photograph this machinery, and identify the date and subjects of the photographs in your documentation.

Maintaining Chain of Custody

Sometimes, your inspections of equipment, devices, or machinery will lead you to evidence that the police have seized as part of their investigation. They may require that you run your tests or make your observations in the police lockup, which is a location for holding evidence to be used in a criminal proceeding. You may occasionally be given temporary custody of evidence from the opposing side. When you receive admitted evidence, which has been given exhibit numbers by the authorities, you must maintain what is called a chain of custody.

TACTIC: Treat a chain of custody as a paper trail for the location of any piece of evidence in a legal matter. The paper trail shows where the evidence was and is, moment by moment, and assures everyone that it is the same evidence that was originally seized.

The chain of custody must be maintained from the moment the authorities first seize the evidence, until the final moment when it may be shown and referred to in a trial. Paper records must document changes in the custodianship of evidence – who transferred possession of the item, who accepted possession, the date of the transfer, the method of transfer, and additional information to identify the evidence precisely. Sometimes, witness signatures are also required.

If the evidence is lost or destroyed while in your possession, you could be held legally and financially accountable. Be careful.

Running Tests

Each specialty field has its own requirements for possible testing, its own protocols, and its own procedures. A key part of your contribution is to understand your field well enough to design each test and then run or witness them. If experts in your field generally rely on third parties to run tests, such as independent laboratories, specify that fact and tell the labs explicitly which tests to run, and how to run them. The legal burden is that the tests are run under conditions substantially the same as existed at the time of the event in question.

If your tests are part of standard protocols or methodologies in your discipline, follow procedures similar to those described in peer-reviewed publications. In other word run tests according to commonly accepted guidelines. If your tests require multiple passes to obtain a series of results or data values, run them enough times to justify the results quantitatively.

TACTIC: *Your expert opinions will rely on the results you obtain from tests. The results of your tests are only as valid as the tests.*

Remember, you may be asked why you ran specific tests, why you used or specified individual parameters, and why other tests were not run. You should be able to explain the logic and methodology that led you to the specific tests, and why the results led to your opinions. If your tests show inconsistencies, you must be able to explain them. If some tests in your industry have known error rates, obtain documentation in advance about them and make sure to correlate observed error rates during your tests with the known industry rates.

If the case focuses on equipment that failed, run tests to explain the cause of the failure, and define your tests to show whether the problems lay in original design, follow-on manufacturing, or even usage by company personnel or consumers. And make sure any equipment used to test other equipment or evidence has undergone regular maintenance and / or calibration if necessary. Obtain detailed documentation of the service and keep this information in your own file folder as well. If an opposing attorney determines that you or your laboratory did not maintain or properly calibrate testing equipment, then the judge may dismiss the results. If the equipment does not require calibration, perhaps because results are relative and not absolute, you should know that so that you can testify to it.

Applying the Latest Methodologies

In the computer field, software and operating systems change regularly. In the construction field, building codes change frequently. In aviation, both planes and avionics change from time to time. Maintaining records of these developments will be useful; some legal matters you face will involve the state of your discipline years earlier. Legal cases sometimes involve equipment that has been operating for many years at company facilities.

Having your own reference materials will allow you to rapidly find information to help with your analyses. This could range from printed copies of articles to copies of journals and magazines to computer files.

At the same time, you should know about the latest published developments in your field. Failing to use the current tools of your trade, or software in your specialty, or technology in your science, may be enough to exclude your opinions from court. To be the best expert witness possible, you must keep your expertise current.

Staying Current

Many specialty fields have their own journals or magazines; stay familiar with published developments in your field to ensure that you can select and use the most recent techniques for research and analysis. Using search engines on the web is convenient to discover the latest research. Current information often appears on websites for companies doing the research before it appears in professional journals.

Taking notes

Take notes on all steps you take during your investigations, but remember not to jot down or scribble premature judgments, opinions, guesses, or observations about people and events. Just write down the facts. Everything you write is fair game for an opposing attorney's questions.

TACTIC: Only write down concrete facts that you observe or gather.

Evaluating Gaps in History or Documentation

When an attorney hires you, you will frequently discover that information about the case is missing. In many cases you can use scientific methodologies common in your field to fill in the gaps.

For example, you might have to apply statistical models to make estimations of data values that fall between known data points. Whatever tool you use, you may not just guess. You have to have a legitimate explanation for how you filled the gaps, and you must document the methodology you use to do so, and that approach must be well established in your field.

Accreditation and Certification

If your specialty has an agency that offers accreditation, it will valuable to acquire that. It is also a good idea to have an accredited laboratory perform your tests. Accreditation is an industry accepted guarantee that the work or tests performed meet previously defined standards of excellence.

Certification is individualized. The certification process is voluntary and usually represents a less intense but still significant process of peer review. A person who receives a certification in his or her field of practice has generally participated in professional study and passed examinations to confirm that they have a set of skills and knowledge. For example, Guidance Software offers certifications to computer forensics specialists. The American Council on Exercise (ACE) offers certifications for personal trainers and exercise instructors.

Some certifying organizations require continuing education in the field. Ongoing study is important in fields that change frequently, such as the computer field.

Has your work been 'peer reviewed'?

In the 1993 Supreme Court case "Daubert v. Merrill Dow Pharmaceuticals," Justice Blackmun said for the unanimous court that an expert's testimony has to rest on a reliable foundation and has to be relevant to the task at hand. He brought up the key consideration about whether the theory or technique used can be or has been tested and subjected to 'peer review' and publication.

TACTIC: Expert witnesses have seen their work rejected and their testimony excluded when they haven't attended to Daubert standards of peer review.

Identify another specialist in your field that the court can treat as a peer. So if you are a biomedical engineer, another biomedical engineer would be a peer, and so on. Your attorney can retain this person to review your work, specifically your expert report. A peer reviewer would provide his own report of findings regarding the content of your expert report. Yes, this may sound like double work, but an increasingly appropriate and valuable extra step. If another expert independently verifies the validity of your work, it will help to ensure the legal admissibility of that work. In addition, this extra step can bring extra credibility to your work. This will further support the relevancy and reliability of your work, opinion, and testimony.

The peer reviewer should submit his report directly to the law firm that engaged both of you. Generally, your attorney will submit your expert report, along with the peer reviewer's report and a CV describing the peer reviewer's background, training, and skills. You should not have any contact with the peer reviewer after the law firm retains him and before he submits his report back to them. Keep the points of this paragraph in mind because, from time to time, you may be hired in a case as a peer reviewer rather than as an expert witness.

Sometimes a peer review is called a third-party review, because the other party may not be a precise peer, but may still be a specialist in a related field of expertise. You should use such a third-party reviewer if part of your testimony includes information that is close to, but not specifically part of, your primary expertise.

Summary of Lesson 5

Conducting an expert investigation requires a meticulous approach to documentation of methodologies used and opinions formed. Knowing how to approach and document your work will strengthen the admissibility of your report and your opinions.

I explained how to best handle evidence, acquire and document new information through interviews and testing, and how to handle incomplete or missing information. Also discussed were important elements such as peer reviews, foundation, chain of custody, and the latest methodologies.

6

Writing an Expert Report

The expert report is a cornerstone of your contribution to the case. It is the primary written piece of work, just as your testimony in deposition or court is the primary verbal piece of work. Before writing your expert report, you will spend time researching, explaining, listening, and meeting. Everything you write down will become the subject of interrogation or discussion.[9]

Realize that some attorneys may use your writings long after a case ends. Bright attorneys will often look to the records of your previous cases to see what you have said, how you have said it, and what mistakes you may have made. These writings will guide them to whether you may be an appropriate witness for them to hire. Then again, they can research your previous statements to use against you. They may look at the way you wrote something, or if what you wrote previously relates to a

---

[9] Expert reports are more common than not, so this lesson is very important for most cases you accept. However, not all lawyers want their expert's opinions to appear in writing because they will have to reveal them to the other side.

current opinion that you're expressing in a new case. Be alert to whether a new case you've accepted leads to an opinion that differs from one you may have expressed in a previous case. An industrious attorney will probably discover any differences and call you on them.

Your expert report will need to meet legal standards. It should be organized, easy to read, professional, and effective. Depending on the complexity of the case, you will have one or more opinions about the subject of the case. You should precede your opinions with your background and qualifications to explain who you are and why you are qualified to present those opinions.

Precisely express your opinions. Explicitly list the information you considered while coming to your opinions, and show which pieces of information directly support those opinions. Explain exactly what steps you followed and/or what technical methodologies you used as the basis for the conclusions you reached. Include required additional information, such as your contact information and your fee schedule.

Consider Clarity, Organization, and Memory

Clear thinking should lead to clear writing and focused opinions. If your thinking is muddled, your report and your testimony will probably sound that way. If you think clearly in your discipline, but have not had practice writing or testifying, brush up on those skills or take a class. Expert reports and presentations need to be well outlined and well written.

Organize and group the information you have amassed in such a way that you can show how you reached your opinion. For example:

- I used and observed this fact or these facts.
- I read this information.

- I researched this additional information.
- I ran these tests.
- I learned this from so-and-so.
- I relied on my own experience, education, and knowledge in the industry, along with my findings in the case to lead to the opinions that I'm expressing in this report.

Do not use technical jargon in front of a group of jurors, a judge, or a group of lawyers. You are not talking to technical peers when you offer up expert testimony. Demonstrate that you can translate the complexities of your expertise and your discoveries into simple English.

First, you want to be understood. You do not want jurors rejecting your opinions because they could not understand them, or because they could not understand your reasons for them. Second, you do not want to burden your attorney with having to take time in court to translate your information into plain English. Third, if you do it right, you will be more believable, more credible, and simply more likable, beyond being a respected expert.

Let's not forget that we do sometimes forget...things. In complex cases, the process can easily take months or even years. It may be a year before you even write your expert report. You may not testify to the content of your report for another year or two. It does not matter how bright you are; memories often fade. Details fade even more quickly. You will not remember everything.

A simple rereading of your own report will refresh your memory before meetings or testimony.

The Importance of Your Choice of Words

You've probably heard the phrase: "it's not always just about you." The expert report is not just an expression of your opinions for your own satisfaction. Before you experience it, you cannot realize how much the words you choose, and the way in which you form your sentences, will affect the legal results. Your attorneys and the opposing attorneys will look more closely at what you say and how you say it than any English teacher you ever had.

Quite simply, your attorney wants to be able to quote things you say to help him make his case. The opposing attorney would love to be able to quote things you say that are either wrong or poorly expressed. He would love for you to provide him with ammunition for cross examination. He wants to hear sentences or adjectives that make you sound uncertain, and that may even enable him to use your words to support opposing points of view.

Similarly, you will have the task of reading the opposing expert's report and looking for weak technical work or wording that your retaining attorney can undermine or attack. Your goal in reviewing the other expert's report is to identify the technical strengths and weaknesses found there. This will help your attorney in his effort to discredit the other expert and/or his work. Knowing what to include in your own expert report should make obvious what omissions or errors to look for in the other expert's report.

Maneuver carefully with your opinions. You must sound sure. You must be confident of your opinion. Don't use hedge words or phrases, a common weakness in expert reports. In your reconstruction of an event, or as the result of your tests and analyses, you may reach a firm conclusion. Say so in your opinion. Do not use words like "seemingly," "potentially," "possibly," "maybe" or even phrases like, "it appears that," "it may be that," or "it usually is the case that." If you use phrases and words like these, I can assure you that your opinion will not be helpful. The other attorney will interrogate you about alternative ways to interpret your opinion. He will use your own hedging phraseology to suggest that your opinion should not be taken as credible or convincing. Why should the jury be convinced if you don't even sound convinced?

By the same token, avoid absolutes, unless a condition about which you are talking is truly a sure thing with no exceptions. Just remember that is rare.

You may wonder exactly how to express your opinion when you do not believe that something is 100% certain, but are confident it is or was true. Here is the answer. The strongest and most acceptable phraseology when expressing each of your opinions is to qualify that you are stating the opinion "...to a reasonable degree of scientific certainty" or "...to a reasonable degree of medical certainty."

Understanding what is Discoverable

When something is 'discoverable, it means that either side in a matter can ask for it and receive it as part of the process of accumulating relevant facts in the case. Your case file is discoverable. This includes all notes, photographs, or exhibits you created for use as possible evidence to clarify your opinions. Have copies made of everything before you offer any testimony.

When I write an expert report, I use my computer and make edits in place so that the result is a single report, with no preceding drafts. If you maintain copies of each successive version, you can expect that opposing counsel will ask you to provide copies of those versions. The opposing attorney will then ask questions about each successive series of thoughts you had that led to every changed word or sentence or paragraph. If you are prepared to deal with that, fine. Otherwise, you will be significantly better off writing only one expert report to have to explain and defend.

If your attorney asks to see a draft version of your report, use the watermark feature of the word processing system you use to mark every page of your report as a 'draft.' In this way, you can claim that you were still thinking through the facts, and had not reached your final opinions when the draft report was written. In reality, your opinions may change while discovery continues in the case.

Be prepared to adjust your opinions as new facts come to light. Opinions often evolve during your work. I prefer to think of it as evolving rather than changing. The longer you wait to complete your expert report, the easier it will be to incorporate new facts into your final opinions. However, if new data comes to light after you've written your report, you may supplement your expert report with a new document in which you augment or change opinions. Naturally, you should include in this supplemental report the bases and the new facts that led to those expanded or modified opinions.

TACTIC: Know that the opposing attorney can ask you questions about anything in your case file. Do not doodle or scribble inappropriate notes about observations.

Federal Rules of Civil Procedure – Rule 26

Your expert, or primary, report is a formal report whose content and structure is addressed in Rule 26 of the Federal Rules of Civil Procedure. This Rule defines the general provisions of the law regarding discovery and disclosure of information in a lawsuit. In section (a)(2)(B), the Rule explains in detail the disclosures that an expert witness has to make in a written report, prepared and signed by you, the expert witness. It says:

> "the report shall contain a complete statement of all opinions to be expressed and the basis and reasons therefore; the data or other information considered by the witness in forming the opinions: any exhibits to be used as a summary of or support for the opinions: the qualifications of the witness, including a list of all publications authored by the witness within the preceding 10 years: the compensation to be paid for the study and testimony: and a listing of any other cases in which the witness has testified as an expert at trial or by deposition within the preceding four years."

In preparing your expert report, you can use the sample report that I've included in Appendix D as a starting structure. You can also decide to use your own structure though I would recommend starting with mine or another professional's as a guide.

When you finish your report, sign and date it, and list any peer reviewers who reviewed your findings and report.

Your Report

The report has to be yours. You have to think out what you want to say, and what sections you want to create in it. After you write your report your attorney may ask to read or review it before you submit it formally. A simple review that uncovers errors in grammar, punctuation, or spelling is not a problem. However, substantive changes such as the suggestion that you add additional text or entire sections to the report can be a problem.

TACTIC: If the opposing attorneys and the court discover that your attorney influenced any substantial content of your report, the court has the right and the responsibility to reject all or part of your report.

In this instance, the attorney may seem solicitous or casual, or may simply suggest 'minor' changes in wording or content. Deciding what constitutes a 'minor change' is up to you. In the end, the expert report has to contain your wording and your opinions. You have to stand behind every word; you cannot honestly accept changes in major content.

The job of coming to an opinion is yours. At most, the attorney may help you with minor phraseology in expressing your opinions.

Background and Credentials

As you can see in my sample report, I include my background and qualifications in Section I. I organize and label the information so that it is easy to see my work and educational experience, plus any other relevant experience that qualifies me to be an expert in a legal matter. You should include in this section the primary things in your background that speak to your unique specialty.

I also refer to an Exhibit A which contains my complete CV and an Exhibit B which contains a list of the cases on which I have previously worked. Both of these summaries of credentials help to qualify me, and I include them as separate attachments to each report. If you have any additional and unique experience or credentials that are not expressly included, you should add a paragraph or two about them.

Exhibits

In Section II, I list additional documents referenced in the report. These are additional exhibits added right after the CV and my previous testimonial experience. In exhibits C, D, and so forth, I list and label other printed documents that I wish to reference in the remaining portion of the report. A short sentence with a meaningful label, along with dates, should be enough to identify each of these exhibits.

Compensation and Contact Information

Section III is the Compensation section, which provides an opportunity to document your fee structure, as required by Rule 26. My fee structure is simply an hourly rate plus expenses. If your fee schedule varies according to what services you provide, or under what conditions you provide them, clarify that in this short section. For example, you may charge a higher rate when testifying or a lower rate when traveling. Your contact information, which you can show in "Section IV: Address" should include your business address, even if that is a home office, and the appropriate business phone number.

Bases and Methodologies

In Section V of the sample report, I include entries for various telephone discussions I had with people in the case, and meetings with additional personnel. Throughout this section, I make explicit reference to every document I read, every folder of information I received, and every CD or DVD or other electronic material I received.

Further, I list every legal document provided to me as reference material for the case. Every report written by other experts or related parties in the matter is also listed, as are any deposition transcripts provided to me. These and any other legal documents should be listed in the category of "data or other information."

Section V should recount people you met, things you discussed, actions you took, and materials you reviewed. It can also include any equipment you used, tests you ran, and reconstructions you made. You can explain in detail any analyses or assumptions you made, and any assignments that your attorney may have expressly given to you.

The intent of Section VI is to make clear that you considered the relevant facts you discovered in the materials listed in Section V and that you then applied appropriate procedures and methodologies to those facts. Altogether, this demonstrates that you understood the issues, the events, and the systems involved, and that the facts and methodologies together contribute to the reliability of the conclusions you drew. If you made use of other exhibits or evidence that you wish to use in subsequent trial testimony, refer to them here. If you have created or intend to create any demonstrative exhibits, make reference to them here as well. This might include graphs, mockups, or any other visual materials that you believe will help you better explain your opinions. You can include demonstrative evidence like this for your eventual testimony as one way to keep the jury's attention and to further enhance your credibility.

Not only can the means justify the end, but they must. In my expert reports, the final section (Section VII) summarizes in boldface each conclusion I've reached and every opinion I will express if the matter comes to trial. To support each opinion, you can refer back to earlier portions of your report, and you can include additional text that further explains the basis for each opinion.

Other Considerations for your Report

If you have had the opportunity to review the opposing expert's report, simply include an entire analysis of the report. Avoid commenting on the validity of any of the expert's opinions, simply look at the work, comment on any errors you find in it, and note any invalid assumptions made that may undermine the validity of a conclusion drawn or opinion expressed by the other expert.

When you are hired for the defendant's side, the plaintiff's expert's report will appear first, and you will read that expert's opinions. While you may not have initially considered some of the opinions expressed, look at each one to determine if it is correct and assess whether the opinion (correct or not) has been fully supported by the facts, procedures, and methodologies followed by that expert. Pay particular attention to whether the expert has overstated the evidence, not just where he might have stated erroneous opinions.

Understand the Law(s) Involved

You are not a lawyer.

TACTIC: Never express legal opinions, either in writing or in testimony. However, understanding the legal elements of your case can often enable you to offer industry knowledge that will support your attorney's efforts.

In the sample expert report, I express an opinion that the source code in question provided no competitive advantage to the plaintiffs. This opinion was a direct result of my having asked my retaining attorney about the laws involved in the case – I would not have realized the importance of competitive advantage otherwise.[10]

TACTIC: Ask your attorney early on about the legal issues involved in the case. What can he or she tell you about how your findings relate to those legal issues?

Don't just stop there. Conduct your own research on the Internet about the legal issues so that you understand any ramifications facing the lawyers. In this way, you can focus your efforts more intelligently.

Alternative Structures to Consider

Earlier, I indicated that my report format is not the only reasonable or acceptable one. Other approaches may turn out to be more readable depending on the assignment. Speaking coaches teach that in a verbal presentation, you should start with an introduction in which you tell the listener what you are going to tell them. You then tell them in the primary part of the speech the main information they came to hear. You end the speech or presentation with a summary of what you told them. This approach is simple, but effective. It ensures that they have a sense of your organization. It makes it easy for the listener to know instantly what you <u>plan to convey</u>, what you <u>are conveying</u>, and if they missed anything, what you <u>did convey</u> to them.

---

[10] In Trade Secret litigation, the law defines the characteristics of a trade secret. One characteristic is that the secret, if maintained, must provide a competitive advantage to the holder of the secret. In our case, the code was available to the public on the Internet and in books and therefore was not a secret in the first place. No special or secret financial advantage exists for anyone who gains access to it. In this case, my industry experience enabled me to offer this additional opinion, which was of great benefit to my retaining attorney.

Similarly, you can begin your report with a section labeled Introduction. Clarify your initial contacts with an attorney or client, and why you wrote the report. If you received an express assignment, clearly state so. For example, was it to attempt to reconstruct a scenario, or to explain the events? Include any references to initial client contacts or attorney contacts.

Include specific references by name or location to any buildings or sites involved in your investigations. If the report is not to be submitted to a court, then open the introductory section with a statement showing the name of the person to whom the report is being addressed, and that the report is in direct response to this client's request. By way of clarification and self protection, restate any instructions you received from this client or attorney regarding the reasons for the report.

Follow this with sections that detail the information discussed earlier in this lesson. Include such things as: the printed or electronic information you reviewed; any meetings and discussions with people, what you received from them that you subsequently reviewed, any tests you made, sites you went to, and miscellaneous observations and discoveries that were made as part of your procedures and methodologies. End your report with your opinions and conclusions.

Depending on the specific assignment that led you to write the report, you might also want to explain what analyses you made, why you did those, and what assumptions you made during your work. Finally, you might make recommendations in addition to expressing opinions as a result of your efforts. At the end of this, you might make your work even easier to understand by including a summary of the key results.

Additional Issues to Consider

Some expert reports can lead to improvements in service, process, construction, or treatment. If your report is intended to be corrective, explanatory, or serve as guidance, then a well written summary section may be enough for a reader. You can end your report with your specific opinions, recommendations or suggestions for corrections or changes to achieve improvements in the future. The rest of your report can serve as additional reading material to further clarify any questions that the reader may have.

Every page of printed evidence in a legal matter receives a unique identifying stamp with letters and numbers. In court, then, experts and attorneys can refer to each page by this unique identification code, or "Bates Stamp." When you refer to the contents of a document in your report, you can refer to the document page's Bates stamp number to guide a reader to a specific page. If a document to which you refer in your report does not have Bates numbers, just include the document as an exhibit to your report. Once submitted, every page of your expert report, including the attached exhibits, will receive their own unique Bates stamp numbers.

Hedging and Disclaimers

Sometimes your expert report is requested before you are able to do everything that you feel is necessary. Generally, you should discuss this with your client or attorney before you submit your report. Otherwise, this sets you up for either having to write a supplemental report later, or having to explain why you did not perform the necessary tests.

However, if you must submit your report earlier than you prefer, say so in the report. If you think more tests are necessary before you can finalize an opinion, include the statement that you plan to do the tests and will submit a supplementary report.

TACTIC: Protect your reputation. Do not finalize opinions before the facts are in, and you have taken all necessary steps.

Experts sometimes include a disclaimer in their contract in an attempt to limit their responsibility. For instance, if you are retained to provide opinions on only a well-defined portion of the case, some facts of the case, by definition, will not be presented to you. A disclaimer enables you to disavow any responsibility for elements of the case that you did not know about or that your work assignment did not include.

In addition to a disclaimer in your retainer agreement, you should also further protect yourself by including a disclaimer in every formal report you write. This can be a simple phrase, such as "the opinions expressed in this report are based solely on the information provided to me, and as listed in this report." Check with your retaining attorney for guidance on the best phraseology to use.

Reviewing your report

The reviewing process is an opportunity to contribute an air of professionalism to your report.

After you finish writing, you will want to just hand over the report. By then you are tired, you have worked for weeks or months on it, and you are finished. But, don't hand it over. It's not ready yet.

While you may be ready for a break, or feel confident that you write well and no review is necessary, your next chore is to reread your entire report, from top to bottom, as both an editor and a critic. Check that all necessary sections appear. The flow and organization of your thoughts should be visible. Everything in your report should be clear, and it should be readily apparent what facts you explored and what steps you took that led to your conclusions. Every conclusion and opinion must follow congruently from the facts you refer to in the report.

So far, that's just content. Let's talk for a moment about carelessness. How impressed are you when you read something in a newspaper or a magazine that includes blatant errors in spelling, or less obvious but real errors in grammar? Look for those in your report. If you are not good at spelling or grammar, use your word processor's spell checker or a grammar checker.

You have been trying to create a professional impression with your work, and trying to develop a good reputation as an expert witness. Why negate this good impression through carelessness in spelling or grammar? Review your report! Some experts ask a friend or colleague to read their report out loud to them. They find that this works very effectively for quickly calling attention to errors.

If your report is long or includes many exhibits, you can bind the entire report with spiral binding, or a three-hole punch notebook with labeled separators. Even simple attention to formatting can create a more pleasing and professional presentation.

As I said earlier, your expert report and your expert testimony are the cornerstones of your work. Your report will stand in your stead for people to read, evaluate, and assess the strength of your opinions and the professionalism of your efforts. The appearance of your report reflects directly on you and your carefulness. It also suggests whether you will be an organized and persuasive witness when called to explain the content of the report during testimony.

Reviewing your Case File

Because everything in your case file is fair game for a subsequent deposition, consider cleaning up your case file. It may include irrelevant pieces of paper and you can discard them if they have nothing to do with the analyses and opinions you express in your report. For example, you probably no longer need menus from restaurants or directions to meetings or even empty pieces of paper from boring meetings at which you learned no useful information. During a deposition, opposing counsel attempts to discredit you in various ways. Irrelevant notes and unnecessary pieces of paper in your case file can provide the opposing attorney a means to do this. After all, why would a consummate professional have meaningless pieces of paper in a case file?

Updating Your Expert Report

Sometimes, for whatever reasons, you find out new information after you submit your report. If the new information leads to any changes in your opinion(s), write a supplemental report explaining the changes to your earlier opinions and how the new evidence led to a new and/or changed opinion.

Summary of Lesson 6

We discussed the importance of the expert report and the information sections that you should include within it, from credentials and exhibits to methodologies and opinions. Your responsibilities for reporting and discovery under Rule 26 of the Federal Rules of Civil Procedure were addressed. You also learned ways to organize and draw on the materials and information you collect during your expert investigations.

This chapter also spoke to the importance of word choices and caretaking in your report writing. Review your report in a variety of ways, examining both the appearance of professionalism as well as your susceptibility to attack later during cross examination. Finally, I explained how to hedge your report if you have not yet had enough time to complete the tests or investigations that you felt were necessary.

7

Understanding Psychology and Legal Tactics

You do not need to be afraid of being an expert witness, but you do need to be wary. Even an inexperienced attorney or one who is not particularly sharp has the home-court advantage and knows the rules of the legal game. You will not always know everything that goes on in that legal setting.

In this lesson, you will learn psychological ploys and legal tactics that attorneys use in both deposition and trial settings. You will probably encounter all of these techniques in one setting or the other, or both, so learning about them in advance will benefit you greatly. Lesson 8 will expand on what you learn here for depositions specifically, while lessons 9 through 12 will concentrate on your testimony in trial settings. You will hear many questions in both settings and you must apply your intelligence and these trainings in the same way whether at a deposition or a trial.

Different Styles of Questions

You do not have to be frightened when facing an attorney but you do have to keep your thinking cap on. Most of the time, your problems will not lie with your mastery of your specialty. You are the expert. The problem, if one arises, is potentially the way in which you answer the lawyer's questions.

Lawyers may not know as much as you do about your subject matter, but they know how to phrase questions that can elicit a poorly worded or poorly thought out answer. You must take care in a legal setting in the same way that you have already taken care to master your area's subject matter.

If a lawyer asks you something that starts with "isn't it true that...," that lawyer is trying to lead you. If a lawyer starts a question with "you've said that ..." and follows it immediately with another question, think carefully about his opening gambit. Though he might only have rephrased something you said previously, he rephrased for his own benefit. You may have to correct his rephrasing before responding to his new question.

You should carefully analyze the question and decide what you need or want to say in response, and even then answer carefully. Maintain your wariness.

TACTIC: When attorneys ask you questions, remember that they do not know as much as you do about your specialty's subject matter. They are often either fishing or bluffing.

If the attorney says something incorrect in his question, briefly explain why it is wrong, demonstrating once again that you know your material. If the attorney asks a correctly phrased question, answer it as clearly and as succinctly as possible. You should rarely elaborate unless and until the attorney asks specifically for you to do so.

Questions That Attempts to Discredit You

You will hear two major classes of questions. The first class attempts to discredit you, either personally or professionally. The second class of question seeks to trick you into either telling the other attorney something useful, or making a technical, legal, or simply verbal error.

Accusations of 'Coaching'

A common tactic that opposing attorneys use is to create the impression that you knew the exact questions and that you were coached with the desired answers. The key word is 'exact'. You have to counter that attempted impression; it's not acceptable to know exact questions and answers that were prepared by an attorney for you. You may know the general subjects for questioning but you must phrase your actual answers during testimony according to the actual questions that you hear. For example, here's a possible sequence of questions you may hear, along with some effective answers:

Q: Mr. Expert, did your counsel tell you the questions he was going to ask before you came here today?

A: We reviewed the subject areas that I would be testifying on.

Q: He told you the questions he would be asking, didn't he?

A: I did not know the specific words in his questions. I knew the general subjects of the questions.

Q: You told him what answers you would be giving, didn't you?

A: Discussing testimony is pretty normal for a pre-trial conference. I just restated the opinions that I would be testifying to in court today.

Attacking your Impartiality

Direct attacks on your honesty or integrity are not as likely as subtle ones. For example, asking how much money you make as an expert witness is a common technique used to create distance between you and the jurors. Attorneys will also sometimes ask whether you always work for the defendants or the plaintiffs in your legal work. Some of you will prefer to work for one side or the other in most of your cases. If this becomes a pattern, you should prepare for attorneys to try to establish that you have a bias toward plaintiffs or defendants in general and in this case in particular.

In the beginning of your expert witness career, much of your work may come from one law firm or even the same attorney. The opposing counsel may claim that you are biased in favor of this attorney. Your best defense here is to reiterate your neutrality in the matter and the thoroughness of your investigation, the reliability of your methodologies, and the objectivity of your opinions.

In order to more easily answer any questions along these lines, enter every testimonial setting knowing the details of your prior casework experience. Know roughly how many cases you have worked, how many times you have testified, and what percentage of the time you have worked for the plaintiffs or the defendants.

Attacking Your Ethics and Your Integrity

Attorneys may try to make the jury perceive that your integrity is questionable. For example, a standard question used to suggest that the other side bought your opinion is:

Q: How much are you being paid per hour to deliver your opinions today?

This misleading question suggests that your 'side' has paid for you to testify in a particular way. You want to tell the jury that you were hired to provide objective opinions about the facts in the case. For example:

A: I'm not being paid to deliver or testify to my opinions. I'm being paid for my time, knowledge and expertise. My opinions are completely my own, and my fees for service are independent of the outcome of the case. My company bills my time out at $300/hour (or whatever the rate is).

If your reputation or expertise leads to well paid expert witness jobs, you may begin to hear questions like this:

Q: At your rate of $300 an hour, Mr. / Ms. Expert, you must testify a lot in court?

If your answer to this question is 'Yes', you have to be prepared for the follow-on allegation that you are a professional expert, doing this primarily if not solely for the money. Your best defense is to redefine the reason for your retention – something like this:

A: I believe I have been retained several times because of my experience and knowledge, as well as my reputation for professionalism and objectivity.

TACTIC: Attorneys can make frontal attacks on your credibility at any time. You should not appear startled by rude or abusive questioning tactics. Jurors will give you the benefit of the doubt if you just calmly and simply correct any misstatement by the opposing attorney.

Questions That Attempt to Manipulate You

Open-ended questions are used to encourage honest expert witnesses to tell more, in simple terms, about subjects that are not easily or precisely phrased by opposing counsel. For example:

Q: What did your attorney tell you to say in response to that question?

Hopefully, you were not actually coached about how to answer a specific question. You will be much better served if you can honestly say:

A: She told me to just tell the truth in response to all questions.

Attorneys sometimes make statements and then ask you to agree or disagree with the statement. Sometimes they ask you to give a simple Yes or No answer to a complex question. If you cannot completely agree or disagree with a statement, say so: "I can't agree or disagree completely with that statement." Leave it to the attorney to decide whether to pursue any additional clarification from you.

Attorneys like to use leading questions, especially with experienced expert witnesses. A favorite is the "Yes/No Deal" question. With this question, the attorney tries to make a deal with you about how you will answer his upcoming questions. It can sound like this:

Q: The jury has been here for a long time and would like to get home as soon as possible. Can you agree to help everyone here by answering my questions with a simple 'Yes' or 'No?'

On the surface, it sounds simple and reasonable. However, you will severely hamper your ability to provide effective answers if you agree. A better response than 'sure' or 'yes' that leaves you total flexibility is:

A: As long as it's possible to do so without misleading the jury, I'd be happy to.

Manipulation can also include offhand assumptions. As an industry expert, it is tempting to use your answers to demonstrate your knowledge of your specialty. An attorney's question may try to use that inclination by including an assumption about your specialty area. For example, he may say something like:

Q: Given that you know about 'so-and-so fact' in your industry, please answer the following question.

If you answer the rest of his question, you are essentially agreeing to that fact, and the jury will assume it is true. In fact, however, the 'so-and-so fact' to which the attorney is referring may not actually be a fact; it may also be a critical point with which the other side will make a point. Additionally, if you agree that this referenced 'fact' is valid in your industry, then you will have admitted it is indeed a fact.

Be careful when answering any questions based on assumptions. Do not accept this assumption clause just because the other attorney says it confidently, unless you know it to be true all the time. You are the expert. You should know if it is 100% true, or only sometimes true.

When lawyers restate one of your earlier answers to a question, they are usually attempting to put words in your mouth. Even if it sounds similar to what you said, the attorney's words may have a different meaning under the law than your scientifically-based words may have meant to you. Listen extremely closely when an attorney rephrases something you said. Think about their phraseology in the same precise way you thought about your own previous statement. You want the record to reflect your technical precision. If the attorney's statement does not correctly and precisely characterize your statement's meaning, just point out the inaccuracy and refer back to your earlier phraseology. Remember that you can ask the court reporter to read back an earlier answer.

Questions That Constrain Your Answers

Opposing attorneys can utilize a number of methods during depositions to limit your value at a possible trial. In a deposition, they can ask you to list everything you know about a particular subject, or all the possible ways you know that something could have occurred. It doesn't matter whether you list three or 13 items in response, the possibility remains that you may not think of everything at that moment. If you do not offer a flexible answer, you may not be allowed to expand upon the list during a later trial.

TACTIC: Whenever you attempt to answer such a list-related question, end your answer with: "that's all I can recall at this moment." That allows you to bring up additional list items later.

Another approach is to ask for only some of your opinions at the beginning of a deposition. If they do not explicitly ask for all of your opinions, and you do not enunciate all the opinions that you wrote in your report, you may not be allowed to express them in trial on the legal grounds that you did not say them during your deposition. Your best approach is to come to your deposition knowing exactly how many opinions you want to express, and the bases and foundation for those opinions. At some point during the deposition, you can specifically present those opinions. For example, you may be asked:

Q: Do you have an opinion in this matter?

A: I have four opinions in this matter. My first opinion is...

You now have the floor to continue with additional opinions. You do not have to say anything beyond your specific opinions until and unless the attorney asks you for the bases of those opinions. You will have the opportunity to provide additional details if the case goes to trial.

Painting You into a Corner

Attorneys like to make the jury dislike or disrespect you, thereby making it less likely that they will accept what you have to say regardless of your findings or the quality of your work. Many questions are attempts to reduce the jury's opinion of you in one way or another, even before you have a chance to express any opinions of your own about the issues in the case.

For example, attorneys will try to ascertain how much time you spend in your industry. A question such as "how much of your time is spent as an expert witness?" is common. If your answer is only 5, 10 or even 25%, then your answer is fine. If the percentage is higher than that, the attorney will make it sound as if you are no longer really an expert or a professional in your field, and that you are no longer in tune with your own science or discipline.

It may well be that you only spend a small percentage of your overall time as an expert witness. When you list other things that you do with your life both professionally and personally, it will be clear that you are not just a "hired gun."

The reality is that as you spend more time as an expert witness, you may earn a disproportionate percentage of your overall income doing so. Being an expert witness sometimes becomes a primary job for those who have retired from their specialty and yet are both good and successful at being an expert witness.

TACTIC: Avoid being trapped into answering questions about expert witness work in terms of percentage of dollars. Answer in terms of what other things you do with your time.

It comes across better if you are doing other things professionally in your life. If you still have a job and work full time, then there is no problem – expert witness roles will only happen once in a while and you will work them into the rest of your professional schedule. If you are an entrepreneur and have control over the way in which you spend your time, then a successful practice as an expert witness may take on a growing role in your overall work life.

Attorneys often try to get you to paint yourself into a smaller corner of your shared specialty than the other side's expert, who you likely will know from networking or simply working in the same industry. A favorite technique of opposing attorneys is to ask you casually if you are familiar with their expert. They might use words like 'familiar' or ask you directly what you know of the other expert's reputation in your mutual field. The attorney is seeking your aid in qualifying his expert. That is not your job; that is his job. A polite response about being familiar with the expert should be enough. Do not go overboard with praise, because that will lend extra credence to whatever testimony the other expert later offers.

Different Styles of Opposing Lawyers

Attorneys can ask many different types of questions in a number of different styles. Be prepared to answer factual questions, and be prepared mentally and emotionally for questions that are intended to affect you in a variety of ways. Some questioning techniques are simply meant to unnerve you. Others are intended to disrupt your concentration. Still others attempt to intimidate you and to weaken your resolve and your confidence. Every attorney wants to draw information from you. Your attorney tries to ask gently for information that he knows you have and are prepared to give. You have more to worry about from opposing attorneys.

The Intimidator

The 'intimidator' will come across with a tone of voice that is strong and authoritarian. He'll sound demanding, sometimes disbelieving, and often as if he knows the answer already. His goal is to create doubt in your own mind that you are correct, and to bully you into apparent uncertainty. He hopes that this will translate into doubt regarding how confident you are of what you have done, observed, or concluded.

Avoid giving in to this ruse. Stay calm, pause briefly to understand fully what he has said or asked, and answer his questions confidently.

A variation on this comes from attorneys who ask questions quickly in order to force you into answering just as quickly. You can slow the pace by answering both calmly and in measured tones. This may unsettle the attorney but the main goal is to settle you down. Unless you are a psychotherapist, the attorney questioning you will be more experienced than you in the psychology and techniques of questioning.

TACTIC: Stay calm, thoughtful, and wary. Control the pace of your answers to stay in control of your own emotions and thought processes.

The Long-Distance Runner

In Federal cases, the law requires that deposition testimony must be limited to 7 1/2 hours, which means that federal depositions usually end within one day. In State cases, the questioning can continue for multiple days, which tires everyone. However, you are the one most at risk from fatigue. Your thinking can become muddled and your energy drained, or you may become more relaxed and less wary. Either can result in your not being able to answer questions as precisely.

The 'long-distance runner' attorney will ask questions about virtually everything in your report. This attorney may ask questions that relate to your specialty but not seemingly directly to this case. He may jump around from one subject to another, attempting purposefully to cause confusion about where his questions are leading and what the next question may be. He may ask you to confirm obvious entries in your CV, such as your education. He may ask you to explain in depth your opinions, and then ask you to clarify each one of your explanations. He may then ask you to elaborate on each one of those clarifications.

First, his intent is to wear you down, in hope that you will misspeak or, through fatigue, fall into one of the trap questions. Second, by having you address similar questions multiple times, you may phrase a different answer to a previously asked question. Then you will be forced to explain discrepancies in your own answers. This weakens your position and undermines your credibility when it comes time to testify. Conflicts in your own answers will not sound credible when trying to explain yourself in front of a jury.

Helpful hint: sip water or juice to stay hydrated. And the better physical shape you are in, the easier it will be to keep your wits about you.

TACTIC: You can ask for a break any time you like. You do not have to explain yourself, although the bathroom is always an easy excuse.

The Buddy

Some attorneys come across as unbelievably friendly; they may even be friendly outside of the legal setting. But remember that litigation is an adversarial process. An opposing attorney in this setting wants you to help him. He may use techniques to trick or trap you to get information from you that will help his case. Being a buddy can simply be one of those subtle traps to encourage you to provide helpful testimony.

The first reason for friendly questioning is to encourage you to become looser in your answers. The tone of voice may encourage you to expand on your answer or to ramble on beyond what the question alone required.

The attorney may nod his head repeatedly to make it seem as if he agrees with whatever you are saying. Head nodding is a technique to keep you talking, just as you would if a friend were nodding encouragingly while you were chatting in a social setting. Without saying a single additional word, he may raise his eyebrows to encourage you to elaborate further. He may just smile at you, and pause after you have answered. He is hoping that you will fill that void by saying more.

TACTIC: Answer questions as simply as possible. Stop as soon as you answer the question. Do not respond to any buddy techniques by saying anything further. Wait for the next question.

The Fighter

In martial arts, it is easier to be the aggressor. You know what punch or kick you plan to throw and you can throw as many as you want whenever you want, aiming wherever you want. Martial artists know that a good defense will not necessarily keep you from being hit eventually. Some attorneys will attack almost everything you say. They may dispute an answer. They may challenge you to give explanations, definitions, and clarifications. They may sound hostile. They may shake their head to express disapproval or disagreement with what you have said. In its own way, this technique encourages you to elaborate or further explain yourself.

The fighter might also use the rapid-fire questioning technique for the same reason as the Intimidator. If this forces you to speak before you think, you will be likely to make mistakes to his benefit. So, slow down.

TACTIC: The best counter to rapid-fire questions is to slow your responses down in a slightly but not demonstrably exaggerated way.

If you do not know the answer to a question, you should simply say: "I don't know." If you just cannot recall information, you can simply say: "I don't remember." If you know where the answer lies, you can ask to see a relevant document that has already been put into evidence. This might be enough to refresh your memory. Don't be surprised to hear questions whose answers you may not immediately remember or even know.

A lawyer in one of my videotaped depositions was this sort of attacking questioner. He frequently leaned across the table at me with questions and physical attempts to intimidate me, while staying just beyond camera range so it was not obvious what he was doing. You can react to this sort of attorney in a couple of ways. First, you can simply respond with civility, cordiality, and politeness, regardless of what you are thinking inside. Just stay calm and keep your eyes on the camera. The judge and jury may later view excerpts introduced from the videotape of your deposition. Looking straight at the camera will make it appear as if you are looking them straight in the eyes, which will come across as more believable.

You can also defuse the pressure a bit by asking for a break in the proceedings. And, your own attorney may object to the opposing attorney's actions or tone of voice. Whatever you do, though, maintain your calm and your composure, and ignore the efforts to disrupt your thinking and your presence.

TACTIC: The night before questioning, get a good night's sleep. During a day of questioning, do not have a large lunch and do not drink wine or beer, either of which can account for slower thinking and faster fatiguing.

The Showman

Many of the best showmen become litigators and have the forum of the trial in which to demonstrate their acting skills. You may be impressed at the flair with which a showman-attorney addresses the jury, the gallery, the judge, and you.

Staying calm and measured in your responses is one reasonable approach to take. However, if you are up to it, more animation in your voice and body language tends to counteract the effect the showman obtains through his mannerisms and movements around the courtroom. Don't go overboard, but don't appear wooden. Bring the juror's attention to you by smiling at them while you answer the questions. Politely and professionally look at the attorney when he asks you each question.

Don't be distracted or dismayed by the showman's antics. That is his job. Your job is to capture the juror's attention when you do respond, and to be convincing with both what you say and how you say it.

The Trickster

Finally, opposing attorneys sometimes keep their toughest questions until close to the end of the deposition day. If you are paying attention to every question and concentrating greatly on your responses, you will be more tired in the afternoon then you were in the morning. If the attorney is not worn out by the end stages of his own questioning, he may now hit you with his hardest questions. They may be questions that are more complex, or contain known difficulties for you, based on the facts in the case.

As discussed earlier a lawyer might restate one of your earlier answers, and ask a follow-up question. If you are tired, you might not recognize the subtle differences between your original answer and the attorney's restatement. Stay alert to any question that includes an obvious restatement of an earlier answer.

TACTIC: Do not accept any attorney's restatement of an earlier answer of yours at face value.

Your Relationship with Attorneys

Interactions with you differ vastly between your retaining attorney and the opposing attorney. On the surface, this may be intuitively obvious. As an expert witness, you have to understand the relationships that exist below the surface.

Working with your own Attorney

You are part of the team that hired you. Your team wants to pull the facts together and best present whatever helps their case. If you testify during a trial, mediation, or arbitration, your attorney-client will ask questions to extract helpful findings from you. You will know in advance of each proceeding the sorts of questions that will be asked and your attorney will know in advance what findings you will present.

When you are answering questions from the attorney on your side, you want to be helpful, not hurtful. Your goal is to simply and clearly present the helpful facts that you have uncovered or the helpful opinions you have come to. A further goal is to elaborate just enough to help the judge or jury understand and to convince them of what you say. Unless explicitly requested by one of the attorneys, do not offer information that you may have discovered could hurt their case. You are only a pawn in the proceedings. The lawyers try to move you in ways that will help them.

If you are objective and effective, then your research and efforts will have discovered both the good and the bad. You need to explain those facts in advance to your attorney-client so that he or she will have all the information needed to decide what is best to present into evidence, and will know which questions are appropriate to ask to ensure that you have an opportunity to express those positive findings. You will not be asked for any of the negatives that you found. That is the opposing attorney's job.

Your attorney is in an interesting position. He has more latitude in a deposition to object to certain questions than he will have in a trial. The posturing and the jousting that goes on between your attorney and the opposing attorney during a deposition may confuse you. You will also be confused when your attorney objects to something and then tells you that you can answer the question anyway. Legal reasons exist for these objections, and the attorneys have to set themselves up for objections that they will use during a trial because they initially expressed them in the deposition. But another reason exists for discussing attorney commentary.

Listen closely when your attorney talks, whether during a deposition or during the trial. During your deposition, your attorney will not speak often. When he does speak, it may be for a legal purpose. However, he may also be attempting to convey information to you. If your attorney explicitly tells you not to answer a question, don't answer the question. Just comment on the record that you are not going to answer the question on advice of your retaining attorney.

During a trial, your attorney will also not say much during cross examination of you by the other attorney. Pay close attention if your attorney objects to one of the cross examining attorney's questions. If you are then instructed to answer, state that you did not understand the question, even if you believed that you did, and ask that it be rephrased. Try to figure out why your attorney objected and what the purpose was behind the cross-examiner's question.

Your attorney may be attempting to convey important information to you. He may be asking the other attorney to clarify something because he senses you will not ask for that clarification; he may know you haven't realized a possible trick in the question. If your attorney does indeed do this, the other attorney will realize this and sparks might very well fly between the two of them. Leave the posturing and the arguments to them, but use the interplay to figure out what advice your attorney is trying to give you.

Working with the Opposing Attorney

Everyone understands which side hired you. Everyone knows what expert witnesses are supposed to do, and they do not expect you to advocate for your side, or be adversarial to the other.

While you can comfortably and persuasively present the positive facts that you have discovered to your attorney in answer to his or her questions, you can tactfully and politely be unhelpful to the opposing attorney during his questioning. Your answers should be, of course, correct and honest. However, they do not have to be expansive. Terse answers will do two things: First, they help to keep you out of trouble, because you will not be as likely to step into traps or to make misstatements. Second, they will make the opposing attorney's job tougher. He will have to think harder, and he will have to ask the right questions to elicit answers and information from you.

Opposing attorneys do not know your expertise as well as you, so they do not always know the right questions to ask. It is their job to find an expert who will help them ask the right questions. If their questions are not complete, that is too bad for them. If their questions are imprecise, that is also too bad for them. You do not, and you should not, help them by correcting poorly stated questions. You certainly do not have to answer a question that they should have asked. You will know if they have not asked the right question, and you will even know if they haven't phrased the right question effectively. You will have to honestly answer any questions that they do ask of you. But if they are not doing a good job as a questioner, you do not have to help them.

TACTIC: *When queried by opposing counsel, shorter answers are best. When you hear poorly worded questions, answer them appropriately, but do not answer the questions you think they meant to ask. Your answers only have to be as precise as their questions.*

Summary of Lesson 7

This lesson demonstrated how lawyers use psychology when questioning you as an expert witness. I explored how attorneys use special tactics to discredit you and your testimony. They also use these techniques to weaken your resolve or to simply trick you outright into undermining the effectiveness of any testimony you offer.

You also learned about questioning styles that you will encounter with different cross examining attorneys. I explained how to identify and respond to them. Dealing with opposing counsels was primary in this lesson, but I also explained how you should interact with your own attorney. Even during questioning by opposing counsel, you can understand and benefit from various psychological and tactical approaches used by your own retaining attorney.

8

Preparing for and Understanding Depositions

Depositions and trials are the two principal forums in which you will be on the hot seat. In both forums you will present opinions that you have formulated and usually have memorialized in an expert report. In both forums, you will hear challenging questioning about your background, your credentials, your methodologies and your opinions. In both settings, other people's fortunes, if not their lives or freedom, will be at risk. The results in a lawsuit depend on both the performance and the conclusions of the expert witnesses regardless of the forum.

Most of the time, lawsuits never get to trial. Civil suits are usually settled. In criminal suits, defendants often agree to 'plead out' to a lesser charge in exchange for giving up and not taking the risk of doing worse at trial.

Most legal proceedings never reach the trial stage, although some obviously do, and others get only as far as the deposition stage. It is an important part of the legal process, and this entire lesson focuses on ensuring that you understand everything about a deposition. I'll explain the elements of a deposition, as well as how to best prepare for it, and how to act during it.

Physical, Mental, and Emotional Preparation

Plan to arrive at your deposition well dressed and well rested. You will be more respected and better treated during the deposition if you look the part, and if you are well rested you will fare better in the physically, mentally, and emotionally fatiguing process. It can go on for hours and sometimes days.

- Physically -- you may not be used to sitting for so many hours. You may develop aches and pains. You may already have physical injuries that will become distracting after several hours of sitting in a chair.
- Mentally -- you will be required to think constantly, not only about the right answers to the opposing attorney's questions, but of the best way to phrase those answers. Beyond that, you will be a better expert witness if you also analyze the intent of each question. It will help if you can think ahead to see where each question or line of questioning seems to lead. Anticipation will enable you to construct better answers and to prepare better for follow-on questions.
- Emotionally -- know that the opposing attorney is seeking to discredit your positions and to undermine your confidence.

Understanding the Deposition Process

By the time the deposition comes around, the process of discovering facts in the matter has largely come to its final phase. By this point, you have probably seen much of the relevant information that has come to light. You have certainly seen the information that relates directly to the opinions you formulated. You will have contributed your own research and investigation to the discovery process to complete your expert report.

The Effects of Your Testimony

The deposition phase of the case usually represents the final stage of discovery. At this point, the discovery concerns more than just the facts in evidence. Behind this factual discovery is the discovery of information about you as a witness in a trial, if one occurs. The question of how effective a witness you will be at trial lies beyond the facts, beyond the opinions that you have formulated, and beyond all the organized bases for those opinions. I have been an expert in more than 100 cases. Most of them settle or end as a result of what is learned during the discovery phase. There's no hard number, but in my experience, no more than 20% of them reach the deposition phase and less than 10% reach the trial phase.

Litigation is expensive and hiring experts makes it even more costly. Both sides would like to settle if possible, and you are a major reason why they may decide to do so. If your work is solid, and you look and sound solid, you will impress the attorneys for the other side as a witness who will be believable and convincing to a jury. They may be more inclined to settle once they realize this. You are part of the discovery process. When both sides discover how much you can help or hurt them, then you become another card to play in this metaphorical poker game.

A deposition is a legal forum in which you offer sworn testimony.

TACTIC: If the matter comes to trial, and you are unavailable to testify, the attorneys can use your deposition transcript in your place. They can read anything they like from it during the trial.

Naturally, your smiling face and convincing personality would be preferable at trial to someone else intoning your words. However, you should realize the import of each of your words when you speak during the deposition.

It All Begins with a Subpoena

A subpoena is a legal document that somebody usually delivers directly to you. The person who does that is called a Process Server. Sometimes, your attorney will receive a subpoena for you. If you do receive a subpoena directly, you should alert your attorney immediately. Either way, receipt of a subpoena constitutes a legal requirement that you appear at the scheduled deposition. Unlike a call for a meeting at work, or request that you attend a lecture, you cannot ignore a subpoena and you must be prompt. Subpoenas are not scary, but they are official.

Generally, knowing that the deposition has been scheduled should get your attention; it's show time. You have done your research. You have prepared your expert report. You have probably received some payment for your services already. Now it's time to show your mettle. The deposition provides your first opportunity to prove how good you can sound and how quickly you can think. Lawyers will be there and so will other people involved and interested in the proceeding. But you are the star.

The subpoena will list obvious information such as your name and the names of the litigants in the case. It will list the attorneys involved, and instructions regarding the time and place where the deposition will take place. Do not panic if the time and place proposed in the subpoena conflicts with something else that is already on your schedule. This happens frequently. Simply tell your attorney that there is a conflict, and propose an alternative date for the deposition. A telephone call or two from the attorney will rearrange a time and place that works for you and for everyone else who needs to attend your deposition.

The subpoena usually spells out in detail everything you should bring with you to the deposition. This includes your entire case file and everything you have in your possession on which you relied during the preparation of your expert report and opinions.

Bringing everything is the letter of the law, but you should consult your attorney as to whether you need to follow the law precisely or whether you can be more pragmatic.

TACTIC: You do not necessarily have to bring everything on which you relied to the deposition.

For example, the list of things you might exclude are copies of other depositions or other reports that have been filed in the case, and copies of electronic media like CDs or DVDs that you have received. The attorneys involved know these materials exist, and they already have their own copies. If the attorneys insist that you bring these things, just ship everything to the law firm and let them bring all of it to the deposition.

Bring anything in your case file that is unique, such as your notes or your invoices in the case. Also bring copies of other documents that you acquired but have not yet been submitted in the case. You can refer to them and the other attorneys will have an opportunity to question you about their contents.

The Purpose of the Deposition

It's a big test, an oral exam. By this point everyone involved has read your report so they already know what you have to say – your process, your conclusions, etc. But they do not know how well you can say it. In a trial, you speak directly to the jury, and the attorneys need to know how well you can do that.

The opposing attorney wants to know how well you understood the case and how sure you are of those opinions. He wants to determine how meticulous your work was and how convincing you will be to a jury when you express those opinions at a trial. The deposition provides the opposing attorney an opportunity to question you about your methodology to expose any flaws in it. It offers him the opportunity to ask you about your reasons for using specific techniques or tests. Depositions give him a chance to test your knowledge and experience to see whether it holds up to scrutiny. It permits him to test whether you hold up under examination. He will look at your personal and emotional responses to questioning. He will look at how easily rattled you are and where your professional and personal weaknesses may be.

He will ask you detailed questions about your expertise, how it relates to this particular case, and what you did during your investigation. If any potential weaknesses exist in your expert report, he will attempt to clarify or confirm those weaknesses. Additionally, he will ask you questions about your procedures and methods, hoping to have an opportunity during a trial to compare your answers during this deposition with your answers during that trial. For your sake, they should be the same.

Careless answering of questions can discredit you later during trial if your statements at deposition conflict with statements that you make in a trial. When you speak in a deposition, you are putting your opinions on the record. At best, conflicting statements make you less convincing to the jury. At worst, they will give the opposing attorney a legitimate opportunity at impeachment. In a legal setting, impeachment is simply a process of disqualification. If the opposing attorney can show to the judge that your professional knowledge is lacking, that your methodology was flawed, that you are biased, or that your claims are unreliable because of conflicts, the judge can disqualify you as a witness. Your efforts, your research, and your opinions will be rejected as unacceptable for presentation during the trial. Your work will have been wasted.

Yes, I mean to frighten you just a little. Depositions are serious business, and you are being paid well. If you have progressed to Lesson 8, then I assume you are serious about wanting to be a better expert witness. As I've said before, you will have to remain calm and thoughtful and exceptionally wary. You are on the defense in a deposition. Although I have a black belt in martial arts, I cannot be 100% sure of the outcome if I were to get into a fight. I have the equivalent of a black belt in expert witnessing after decades of experience, but I am still cautious when walking into a deposition.

TACTIC: Let confidence comfort you, but let caution guide you!

Preparing at a Pre-Deposition Conference

The pre-deposition conference is a fancy term for any meeting or telephone conversation you have with your retaining attorney during which you discuss the upcoming deposition. Specifically, you should discuss the likely scope of questioning from the opposing attorney, and your attorney can help prepare you to answer more effectively.

You and your retaining attorney should always have such a preparatory conference. A conscientious pre-deposition conference with your attorney should be second nature to a well-prepared and well organized team. Unfortunately, you will often have to urge, encourage, and sometimes even force such a conference. If the week before the deposition arrives, and you cannot easily answer the following questions, then you need that pre-deposition conference.

- Which documents does your attorney believe are the most helpful or the most harmful to your side's overall presentation and position? What are the main points that were made in those important documents? Do they support or contradict the opinions expressed by you or the other expert? Who wrote, received, or distributed those documents, and what are their responsibilities in the organization?
- What issues most interest the opposing attorney?
- Which of your opinions are the most important to the case?
- What other information specific to the case and your expertise should you incorporate into your answers during deposition testimony?
- Which of your opinions is most likely to draw the greatest fire from the opposing attorney? Where does your attorney think the strongest attacks on you and your opinions will come from? Have clear and solid explanations of why those potential attacks or proposed alternatives should be discounted.
- On which other facts or opinions in this case (such as opinions expressed by the other expert in his report) does your attorney want an additional opinion from you? Not only should you be prepared to comment on anything the other expert has written, but you should

discuss the importance to his case strategy of such comments. At times, your testimony will negate or minimize the validity of the other expert's opinions. To whatever extent possible, you should prepare to do so at your deposition. Understand your attorney's plans, tactics, and strategies, at least to the extent he will share them with you.

- One final open ended question: "what else is important for me to know, prepare, or anticipate?"

You cannot answer these questions in a five-minute walk to the deposition from your attorney's office, or in the half-hour coffee and cake before the deposition.

TACTIC: If you have not gotten answers to these bulleted questions in a pre-deposition conference, call your attorney on the phone and ask the questions.

Attorneys sometimes ask questions that seem casual, or as if they are simply trying to understand the technical facts. In many cases, they are actually trying to determine how you might answer such a question in the deposition. If you are unsure whether you're being given a mini-test, or simply being asked a question, ask.

Protecting Other Cases You May Be Working on

Often you will work on more than one case at a time. Occasionally, one of those other cases will have required you to sign a confidentiality agreement regarding privileged information, or you may even be expected to maintain confidentiality regarding the very existence of that case. During depositions, the other side can question you about your other work. Discuss these issues with your attorney prior to the deposition.

Deposing attorneys will often ask you questions about your concurrent cases. To maintain confidentiality, your retaining attorney must seek a protective order for your testimony before the deposition. Put the burden on him or her to take care of that for you.

Working toward Settlement

Your credibility is built not only on your fair and objective investigation, but on a fair and reasonable approach to the facts. This means that while you may hold strong to your own opinions, you need not fight against every opinion expressed by the other side. Accepting some opinions or facts that do not conflict directly with your own opinions will enhance your credibility because of your apparent reasonableness.

We have already discussed credibility with the jury. Credibility may affect a verdict if a trial occurs. In a deposition, you want the opposing side to know that you have performed a thorough analysis and that you have reached fair and objective opinions. If you convince them that you will probably present those opinions effectively at trial, you will have increased the likelihood of a better and earlier settlement for your client as well.

Describing the Deposition Setting

Depositions are like conferences or small meetings. The side that has subpoenaed you will generally hold a deposition at their law offices and anywhere from 4 to 20 people will be there. Each side has to have at least one attorney present. Other attorneys may be there for specialized purposes, especially in a complicated case involving multiple litigants. Usually, each side will bring one to several additional interested people, including the clients who originally hired the attorneys.

Sometimes an opposing expert and one to several employees of the opposing client's company will attend in order to check the accuracy of what you have to say. Finally, the Court Reporter will be there. He or she is a licensed professional who will type in legal shorthand a recording of every word that is spoken during the deposition proceedings.

Do not offer your office or your home as the site of your deposition. Other files and computer contents at those sites may be discoverable and you may be expected to allow access to them during your deposition. Let the attorneys find a space.

After you arrive at your deposition, and before it begins, the opposing attorney will ask if you brought your case file with you. Not only should you have brought it with you, but you should have read everything in it to refresh your memory. The opposing attorney will ask questions about anything that he finds inside your case file.[11]

Your file folder should only contain information that you relied on to form your opinions. Do not take a laptop computer or an attaché case or any other documents with you. The opposing attorney could ask to look at those things.

Opposing attorneys will generally start by copying your file folder and its contents so they can refer to the copy during the deposition. You can refer to your original papers, referencing exact contents during questioning. If your file is extensive, it may take a while to make this copy, and the opposing attorney may

---

[11] You should have shown that entire case file to your attorney before arriving at the deposition. If your file has any privileged information in it, your attorney has the right to remove it before the other attorney has the opportunity to copy it and ask you questions about it.

begin the deposition without the copies or your originals being available. When this occurs, they generally begin with an innocuous set of questions that address your background, experience and education.

An important point here is that you will not always have your CV in front of you to quote from or to refresh your memory about your own background. However, if you do not remember the details and dates, say so, and say that you would like to wait until your CV and case file have been returned to you. You do not want to omit entering into the record important facts about your background, experience, and credentials. An important reason for asking about your background is to validate that you have the training and specialized knowledge of your field that is required to qualify as an expert witness.

TACTIC: Review everything in your case file, which should include an updated CV, before you arrive at the deposition.

Once the deposition begins, the Court Reporter will swear you in just as you see on television in a trial. At that point, the opposing attorney will usually begin the proceedings by asking you for your full name and ask you to spell it for the record. If you are new to testimony, he or she will surely offer you a brief explanation of the process, and then ask if you understand and if you have any questions. Obviously, ask any questions that you do have at this point.

After you have been deposed several times, the opposing attorney will probably comment on that fact and skip over any lengthy explanations of the process. Some attorneys and experts suggest that you ask the opposing attorney to review explicitly the ground rules that you should know, even if you have been deposed many times in the past. Rules can change from time to time, or from state to state.

If the deposition proceeds and your case file has not yet been returned to you, you may not recall the details needed to answer the opposing attorney's questions. Do not work from memory. Simply say that a necessary piece of information is in your file and you will be glad to address the question when your file is returned to you.

The Job of the Court Reporter

During any breaks agreed on by both attorneys, the Court Reporter will stop typing. At this point, you are "off the record." When the proceedings continue, the Court Reporter will continue typing and you will be "back on the record." The court reporter also has the task of marking and identifying each new piece of evidence before you begin answering questions about its contents. The opposing counsel can either bring a new document or exhibit to the deposition or he may introduce into evidence a document that you brought as part of your case file.

If you are asked questions that are unclear because the attorney's phraseology is not clear, say so and ask for a rephrase of the question. If, however, the question was complicated and you just lost your concentration, which does happen from time to time, don't let that bother you, but do not admit it either. Just ask the court reporter to reread the question. If the attorney asks you a question that you recall being asked earlier, you can ask that the previous question and answer be reread by the court reporter.

If you notice that you are requesting a rereading or a rephrasing too often, it may be time to take a break.

What Can You Expect from the Opposing Attorney?

Be prepared for open ended questions. If they have learned well, deposing attorneys will probably jump right to your opinions, have you enunciate each one, and then ask you to tell them what you did to reach each of those conclusions. For each opinion, they may repeat the same sequence of questions: what *exact procedures* did you follow, Mr. Expert? Can you explain those steps further? They may well ask what steps you did *not* pursue, and *why*? Can you tell them about the *results*? For each result, they may ask you to describe in detail *how that result affected each opinion* you offered. They will ask open-ended questions about what *assumptions* you made in your explorations. In all cases, they are hoping that you will ramble on enough to give them useful additional information.

Be prepared as well for additional, related questions, such as:

Q: "Who chose the materials you reviewed, Mr. Expert?"

You should have received preliminary material from your retaining attorney to review. After you review this material, you are then free to ask for and choose additional materials to review.

Q: "Ms. Expert, what else did you consider in your opinions but eventually decide not to rely on?"

Be careful in your response because you have to have solid reasons (like irrelevance) for having excluded something from your final opinions. The reason cannot be that the material would help the opinion of the other side in the matter.

Attorneys learn to ask these starter questions of almost every witness. Other questions exist and I'll cover the principal additional ones in Lesson 9.

What Do They Want from You?

The opposing attorney, his client, any other attorneys in the room, the opposing expert, and any techie on the other side of the table want to know how much you know. Some of them will have read your report, and so they will know roughly what you are about to say. They may not know all the details since none of them will have seen your notes yet. Most of them will not have read the documents or materials that you used during your investigation and referenced in your report.

The deposition is their first opportunity to get a look at you. They want to measure you. How do you look? How do you sound? The lawyers will be assessing what effect you will have on the jury if the case goes to trial. The client on the other side of the table wants to know if you are a better expert than their expert, if you know more than their expert, and if your assessments are correct or not. They want to know if you are better able to present the technical elements of the case than their expert.

Perhaps, they just want to know whether you are an honest expert whose opinions will help reduce the extent of their success in the case. Then again, if they know that they are on the wrong side of the facts, they will want to know if you have the proof against them. They will assess whether you have done a professional job in coming to your conclusions, and if you have the ability to sway the jury into accepting those results.

In short, everybody wants to discover as much as possible about you. Your knowledge and experience supports your qualifications to do the job, legitimizes the opinions you offer, and suggests how strong a witness you will be when presenting those opinions in a trial.

TACTIC: The strength or weakness of both sides of the case depends not only on the facts in the matter, but on the expert's ability to present analyses and opinions to the 'triers of fact.'

The phrase 'triers of fact' refers to the people responsible for the final judgment of the case. This may be jurors, or it may be a judge alone in a trial that does not involve jurors. When a judge alone reviews all evidence in a trial and decides a verdict without any jury, it is called a 'bench trial.' The participants in the litigation may also have agreed on the use of an arbitrator or mediator who may have similar responsibilities to these more recognizable 'triers of fact.'

The Other Side Wants to Discredit You

Keep in mind that the deposition process may be presented to you as simply a discovery process. Attorneys have said to me in deposition that they are just "trying to learn the facts." That statement is sometimes an attempt to cause you to drop your guard and to be more relaxed than you should be. Yes, they are trying to get the facts out, but that is not all they are trying to do. An unstated goal of the deposition day is to somehow get you to put statements on the record that may later be used to embarrass, discredit, or disqualify you.

A key goal of the opposing attorney, through the intensity and thoroughness of his questioning, is to uncover any outright mistakes, notable weaknesses, or notable oversights that you may have made during the process of your investigations. In addition, the opposing attorney may ask you questions from different angles at different times during the deposition day. He is hoping that you will give answers that may be different enough that he can claim later at trial that they sound contradictory.

Many lawyers will use the deposition room as a battleground. If possible, they would like to destroy you as an expert witness then and there. A deposition is often the only opportunity you will have to testify in most of your litigation support jobs. The rules here are looser for the attorneys, and they can get away with more risky questioning of you than they would be allowed to do in a trial.

You must stay focused and stay alert in a deposition. Most of the time, your deposition testimony will be the only testimony you give in the case, and its strength and your preparedness can dramatically affect the results.

Defending Yourself with the Little Things

The simplest answer in a deposition is usually best. "Yes." Or "No" is excellent, if the question reasonably allows you to answer that way. Make the opposing attorney work to get information from you. For example, suppose you spent six hours on site running 22 tests that resulted in five new findings, and one final opinion. If the attorney during a deposition says something like "so you ran tests that day," do not just jump in there and spend the next hour describing the tests and the results. That was not even a question; no answer is needed. A pause at this moment will probably force the attorney to say something like "isn't that right"? That is a question and your answer to that should be "yes" and nothing else.

The next question may be: "So, what tests did you run?" Now you can tell them about the tests, but not necessarily about the results. Wait for another question about results. Listen carefully to every question and only respond with what is necessary to answer that specific question.

TACTIC: The simplest answer in a deposition is usually best. "Yes" Or "No" is excellent, whenever possible.

We've already covered how you should dress; be professional.

Get to the deposition office early and choose a seat, if possible, that puts your back to any large windows. Let the people on the opposing side of the table have the glare in their eyes during the day. If you get there too late, don't hesitate to ask if anybody minds if you sit on that side of the table. It will be distracting and fatiguing if you have to look into the sun during a deposition.

During breaks, be polite, but don't socialize. If you discuss the case with your attorney during a break, the content of that conversation is discoverable and the deposing attorney will ask you about it after the break.

Keep your eyes primarily on the questioning attorney, and do not glance at your attorney before you answer questions. That suggests that you will be weak at trial as well, and may not be able to stand up to tough questions without looking to the aid of your own counsel. However, even though you focus primarily on the questioning attorney, your peripheral vision can still take in other forms of information. Keep your mind and your eyes wide open.

If you must refer to a document in your case file, use its Bates-stamp number, along with any title the document may have. Sometimes the same or similar documents are entered into evidence and identifying pages by their unique Bates numbers ensures certainty about which item you are testifying.

Attorneys are good at identifying your use of words like "always" and "never." Remember, few things are <u>always</u> or <u>never</u> true, so do not use those words in your descriptive responses. Attorneys are also good at catching suggestive phrases, like "to tell the truth" or "honestly." And jurors will probably question the honesty or truthfulness of your answers that begin with phrases like those.

At the end of any testimony, whether in a deposition or in trial, you want to leave the deposition room or the witness box in the same confident manner that you entered it. Even if you feel battered, embarrassed, dismayed, frustrated or angry, you do not want to give that away to anybody – not the other attorneys, not the jurors. Keep in mind that everything, even down to the way you walk out of the room at the end of the day, tells an observer something important.

Helping Your Own Attorney

Legal maneuvering begins much earlier than the trial itself. Lawyers frequently file arguments or motions to the judge in almost every case. During the deposition, your own attorney will occasionally object to a question.

TACTIC: Stop talking if your retaining attorney makes an objection.

Get into the habit of pausing for one to two seconds before you begin any answer. This pause helps your attorney because it gives him the time and the opportunity to object if he likes. If you are instructed not to answer, do not answer no matter what arguments the attorneys may get into.

Sometimes you may not be able to attend the trial for which you have been preparing for many months or even years. The burden would then fall to your retaining attorney to convince the judge that your deposition testimony should be admissible. Admissibility is a complicated legal arena. To help your attorney, and because of the increasing importance of Daubert criteria, it becomes crucial that you make the effort to incorporate information about both relevance and reliability into your deposition testimony.

The key criteria, known to attorneys by the acronym PEAT, are important enough to repeat here for you:

- Can you cite any *Peer-reviewed* publication in which the methodology you selected has appeared?

- Does the methodology have any known *Error* rates?

- Is the methodology generally *Accepted* in your field?

- Can you replicate the results if you repeat the *Testing*?

Answers to these questions are important, but are not sufficient. When you express your opinions in deposition, make clear that you used reliable methodologies to reach those opinions. Your testimony must also make clear that your methodologies and approach to your investigations are generally accepted in your particular field. The Daubert and follow-on cases have helped to define admissibility of expert witness testimony. Your testimony must convince the court that your opinions flow logically from the findings based on your chosen methodologies. This could involve additional considerations, such as whether the data used in your investigations and analyses were both qualitatively and quantitatively sufficient to justify your final opinions.

Helping the Court Reporter

The court reporter tries to transcribe accurately what everyone says. If you or anyone else in the room speaks too quickly, this can be difficult. Speaking in measured tones makes the court reporter's job easier, and makes it more likely that the transcript of the deposition will be more accurate. In addition, speaking more slowly than usual can help you to formulate your words more completely and thoughtfully.

TACTIC: The words you say in a deposition and the construction of those words are important because they may be quoted in a later trial. You should use correct grammar, phraseology and facts when you speak in a deposition.

The pace at which you speak in a deposition will not be heard in a court of law, unless the deposition happens to be videotaped. Sometimes, your sphere of expertise has to refer to acronyms or proper names. Whenever you use an uncommon word, you can help the court reporter by spelling it.

It is also important to use simple "Yes" or "No" responses, rather than just shaking or nodding your head. While the court reporter listens to what you say, he or she cannot easily determine what your head movements mean. Finally, do not speak while someone else is speaking. Hearing two voices speaking at the same time is difficult for anyone to understand.

When you first enter the room, give your business card to the court reporter to help with the spelling of your name, as well as the address to which the copy of the transcript can be sent for your review.

Generally, court reporters edit their reports before submitting them for your review. They correct for grammar and spelling, but cannot correct technical misunderstandings regarding your content. That is your job. Remember the court reporter's typed record is a legal document. It assumes even more legal import when you sign that the transcript is a valid reflection of what you said during the deposition.

When It's Over

It is not over until all the attorneys in the room agree that it is over. They have to tell the court reporter that they are now "off the record." You cannot relax until that moment. Sometimes you may hear an attorney say "that's all I have;" you might think that the deposition is over at that point. It rarely is. Any of the other attorneys in the room can still ask additional questions. Even the attorney who said he had no more questions can come back and ask you more, so do not take that proverbial deep breath and relax until the process itself is "off the record" and the deposition officially ends. Depending on the urgency of the case, the attorneys may press the court reporter for immediate copies of the transcript. They may even ask for an electronic 'raw' copy of the deposition. The term "raw" refers to a copy of exactly what the court reporter has typed during the deposition day or days.

After the deposition ends, read the transcript that is sent to you and submit any corrections, which will be incorporated as part of the final confirmed transcript. You may not change any details of opinions; only correct any obvious misunderstandings of the words you spoke during the deposition. If the court reporter thinks he heard something, and you know you did not say the words recorded, you have to catch that. Otherwise, if it is a particularly important phrase regarding your work, you will have allowed a conflict to remain in the record and you will surely have to explain that conflict later at a trial. Do not put yourself in that potentially embarrassing predicament. Spend the necessary time to reread your own transcript and edit any errors before they are cast in stone.

TACTIC: Do not allow your attorney to waive your right to read, review, and correct any errors in the deposition transcript.

Confidentiality Before, During, and After the Deposition

In many legal matters, you will have to sign a confidentiality agreement before you begin work on the case, often before you ever see your first piece of evidence to review. That confidentiality agreement binds you from revealing anything you learn in the case, especially private details. If information becomes public later, perhaps revealed as the result of a trial, then those facts are obviously no longer confidential. However, it is ethically and legally prudent to refrain from discussing the details of your cases with others in the public, such as colleagues, friends or students.

Even after the case is over, be circumspect and guarded about the details of the case. Many of your cases will settle for undisclosed reasons and under unrevealed terms. You played an important role in leading to that settlement. The information you discovered, learned, or concluded may be an important reason for the agreement and settlement by the litigants. You should keep everything you know about the case to yourself.

Summary of Lesson 8

This lesson focused on the details of a deposition, from the initial subpoena to preparing and participating in the deposition. I emphasized the importance of a pre-deposition conference, and laid out a range of preparatory questions and answers for you and your retaining attorney to discuss.

I went over the mechanics of the day and the overall purpose of the deposition; from copying case file information to what you can expect from the deposing attorney. The lesson covered, as well, how to best defend yourself against the efforts of the opposing attorneys.

I also discussed your relationship with the attorneys in the room, especially your own, and demonstrated several ways you can help yourself, your retaining attorney, and even the court reporter.

9

Frequently Asked

Testimonial Questions

Giving testimony in a court of law or in a deposition is a form of speech that has rules. This lesson focuses on answering questions and giving testimony in either a deposition or a trial.

You need to know much more about lawyer's wordplay. In this lesson, you will learn styles of questions you will encounter as an expert witness and effective approaches to take in your answers. Knowing these in advance will help prepare you for the questions in a trial with live jurors, real money, and sometimes real lives in the balance.

Top Testifying Pluses and Minuses

I would like to start by introducing a series of Pluses and Minuses for your answers in trial testimony. These pluses and minuses have to do with your content and the delivery of your content.

<u>Pluses</u>:

- Bringing your ethics with you to a trial. This includes maintaining objectivity and presenting facts fairly.

- Delivering your answers in simple English, even when the questioning attorney asks you questions using acronyms or industry terms.

- Answering questions honestly, even if those answers do not help your side of the case.

- Maintaining an air of calmness and composure at all times, when you answer a question, when you listen to a question, and even when a cross examining attorney demonstrates occasional rudeness in a question.

- Recognizing the limits of your own expertise, and only answering questions within that scope of knowledge. Do not allow an attorney to cajole you into stretching what you know and commenting casually on something beyond your expertise.

- Answering politely and briefly, even when the cross examining attorney uses body language or voice control to encourage you to expound further.

<u>Minuses</u>:

- Losing your composure under harsh questioning. You will maintain your professional credibility with the jury if you respond to all questions — simple or complicated, casual or rude — with both calmness and composure.

- Speaking in technical terms to the jury. They will either become bored or not understand your work. You have to speak in plain English, and you have to interpret your work in plain English for them.

- Acting superior or arrogant because of your expertise or position in life.

- Arguing or using sarcasm with the cross examining attorney.

- Exaggerating good points for your side. You can, however, clarify or emphasize the strength or weakness of points of fact.

- Answering questions that force you to reach beyond your professional comfort zone. Guesswork falls into this category. Do not ever guess during testimony. You are there for expert knowledge. Nobody expects you to know everything, so if you do not know something, even about your specialty, just admit it.

- Taking a case that is outside your field of expertise.

TACTIC: Exaggeration undermines believability.

Characterizing Testimonial Answers

The easiest answer, but the one that requires the most care, is a simple and truthful response to the precise question asked. During this lesson, I will assume the role of the student to help you learn how to exercise that care, and to provide answers that will help the court and not hurt you or your side in the matter.

In no particular order:

- Answer questions that begin with, "do you know..." or "are you familiar with...?" with a simple "Yes" or "No." Answer yes only if you really do know.

- Do not guess about what else the attorney may want or where that opening query might lead. Wait for the follow-up question that will hopefully clarify that.

- If you really do not know, or you are not sure, then say "I don't know." Nothing else. Do not offer any explanation of why you do not know.

- If you think the statement is true but you are not sure how or why you seem to know, you are probably still best served by answering. "I don't know." Generally, if you assert that you know a fact in your field of expertise, the questioning attorney will then ask you "how exactly do you know that, Mr. Expert?"

- The simplest of factual questions only require the simplest of factual answers. For example, "how tall was the building?" requires only a numerical response, such as "175 feet." Do not offer any additional information about the building, such as: "... and it was made out of brick, had double pane windows, and was only six years old." You are asking for trouble by offering unrequested additional information.

- If you offer unrequested extra information, you will almost always receive follow-up questions. You may be asked about materials such as brick, or single versus double pane windows, or aging of the building. The attorney is entitled to ask you additional questions about every word you incorporated into your response until he is sure that nothing valuable or relevant remains to be learned. More often than not, your expanded answers will lead to useful information for the other side. The net effect is that you will have done your side a disservice.

- You will not recall some facts that you once knew. Just say so: "I don't remember." If subsequently asked why you do not remember, you can say that the answer lies within your notes, or your report, or an exhibit you read. You could then ask to see the piece of evidence that you know contains the answer.

TACTIC: Never speculate in an answer!

- Speculation is allowed during a deposition, and you may be invited to do so by an opposing attorney, but you should never speculate in answer to any question. If an opposing attorney quotes your speculation during a subsequent trial, he can make you sound less sure of your investigations or facts. Speculations offer the cross examining attorney an opportunity to suggest that the jury should consider your speculations as legitimate alternatives. Do not allow yourself to be manipulated.

- Finally, if you do not understand a question for any reason – you misunderstood it, or it has many clauses – do not try to answer. Your best answer is simply "I don't understand your question." Leave it to the questioning attorney to decide whether to rephrase or move on to another question.

A common error occurs when a question uses familiar terminology in an unfamiliar way. If you ask the attorney: "Which of several possibilities do you mean?" and show off by listing them, the attorney will then ask you to give answers for each of the possibilities. Alternatively, you will be at the beginning of a new sequence of questions about each of those possibilities. For example:

Q: Mr. Expert, the plaintiff is alleging that his medical records were still available online, even though they were supposed to have been removed from the doctor's database. Can you explain that?

The use of the word 'removed' is vague from a technical perspective. You should force the questioner to clarify it. You should never offer the questioner multiple possibilities from which to choose. If you do that, you will likely be forced down each of those paths.

Bad Answer: First, 'removed' could mean 'purged' or 'deleted,' which have different meanings in computer technology. Even 'deleted' has a variety of meanings when one looks at computer storage from a forensics perspective. Which of those possibilities did you mean?

Good Answer: I don't understand the question.

If you simply answer that you did not understand the question, the attorney will probably ask this follow-on question:

Q: What part of my question did you not understand?

Your best follow-up answer is a simple yet focused:

A: I didn't understand what you meant by 'removed' in your question.

TACTIC: If you are not sure of what the attorney means by a question, say so!

Sample Q&A -- the Good, the Bad, and the Ugly

Lawyers use the same questioning techniques in both depositions and trials, and you should learn to use intelligent responses as well. Let's start with a few examples.

Q: Mr. Expert, would you state your name for the record?

A: My name is John Q. Expert, I live at 15 Central Ave., Ashland, OR 97520, my phone number is 949-555-1467, and I work as a sole proprietor under the name 'Computer Options.'

Observations: that was the 'Bad.' You may think that they will ask for those things anyway, so why wait? You were only asked for your name, yet you gave an address, a phone number, and information about your business. You were only asked for your name. That is all you should have given.

Here is what the other lawyer gained from that response. In what was probably the first question of the deposition or trial, you gave away your inexperience completely. You showed that you do not listen carefully to questions, you not only answer the question asked, but you give much more information than required. You are probably going to be an easy mark during the rest of the testimony. Your own attorney is already cringing, and the other attorney knows that you are going to make his job much easier and help his case.

Here is a good example from a deposition:

Q: Mr. Expert, do you have an opinion about why the building collapsed?

A: Yes.

Q: What is the basis for that opinion?

A: My entire investigation of the case.

Observations: those answers are the 'Good.' Nothing extra was given and the attorney has to decide whether to probe further. He may decide not to, choosing to rely on what you have already written in your expert report. That allows him to move on to other areas, and allows you and your attorney to avoid telling any more at the deposition, saving it for trial.

Here is an ugly example:

Q: Did you study the contents of the hard drive?

A: I sure did. That guy's so guilty I can't believe it. He had more than 700 pictures of pornography on his computer, there were more than two dozen searches for information about hunting knives, just like the one that was used in the murder, and there was an entire chat room full of conversation about terrorist plans.

Observations: that was the 'Ugly.' Your answer should once again have simply been "yes," until you heard what other questions were asked about your study of the hard drive. Here is what the other lawyer gained:

First, you disclosed three significant things you did – namely, finding pornography, discovering Internet searches about weaponry, and discovering chat room conversations about terrorist plans. Those unrequested admissions provide the opposing attorney with three new areas about which to ask you questions, areas he may not have been planning to venture into. Worse, those three areas may provide no support for the real opinions that you planned to offer to the court. You may end on the defensive for even having been asked to look at particular information.

Second, you made a legal judgment by saying that the defendant was guilty. That may be your opinion, but you have no legal right to say it. This will be addressed below in more detail.

TACTIC: You are not qualified to offer a legal opinion; you are only qualified to bring your expertise to the court. Do not make legal assessments or judgments.

Defusing the Compound Question

During questioning, attorneys will sometimes ramble on with long questions that include multiple clauses. Parts of these questions may be assumptions, other parts may be questions, and still others may be comments by the attorney. The result is a vague invitation by the attorney for you to respond with a similarly rambling and possibly revealing answer of your own. Here is an example, with an experienced response:

Q: Mr. Expert, considering the details of this case and the research you have done, what is it that you are really saying and how do you explain your conclusions?

A: That was not clear; there seem to be multiple questions there.

Observations: That was good. You conveyed to the attorney that you understood his attempt to present a vague and compound question to you. You were polite, and the ball is back in his court.

Continuing with the probable follow-up:

Q: Which part of my question was not clear?

A: I would appreciate it if you could break your question down into individual questions. I will be glad to answer each one as well as I can.

Observations: that was a good comeback. If you answer a compound question, the attorney can use your answer to apply to any portion of the question. You buy into the vagueness as well as possibly any assumptions that the attorney phrased as part of the complex question. The attorney can make it sound like you have answered all parts of his compound question with your single answer.

TACTIC: Some compound questions are subtle and may sound like a single question. Ask attorneys to restate compound or vague questions in simpler form for you to answer.

For example, "have you stopped embezzling from your employer?" Even though it sounds like a single question, this question has two parts; namely, whether you were embezzling previously, and whether you are still embezzling. Again, listen carefully. Ask for a restatement of the question if you are confused or suspect wordplay. If you can identify a question as compound, simply say so and ask for a clarification.

Attacking the Factual Basis of Your Testimony

I would like to demonstrate for you a series of standard questions that attorneys ask. You should readily see how they can apply to you, and what you can do to avoid being undercut by these kinds of questions. I will pair each question with commentary about what the attorney wants to accomplish and what a juror may think when he hears your response. The attorney may well achieve his intent to damage you if you do not adapt your preparations effectively. You should let these questions guide your preparations when collecting information for your next case.

> Q: Did you interview the patient?   <u>Or</u>
> Did you go to the scene?   <u>Or</u>
> Did you go to the factory?

<u>Commentary and possible juror thoughts</u>: The answers should be yes. How familiar can you be with the victim, or the scene of the crime, or the product in question, if your research or investigations never took you there? Go where you need to go to learn your own facts directly. First-hand knowledge is best!

Q: Did your tests follow any authoritative industry protocol?

Comments: Again, the answer should be yes. If not, the next thing you hear may well be the claim that your procedures are not scientific. If such a protocol exists in your industry, you should have followed it.

Q: Did you do any testing?   Or
   Did you take measurements?

Comments: If you did not run tests, the next question you hear will be: "why not"? If you did run tests, you may hear attacks on precision, accuracy, or reliability of your measured results. Perform necessary tests and take necessary measurements. You should have explanations ready to support your claim that the results were precise, accurate, and reliable.

Q: Isn't it true that the tests you conducted have no established industry standards or protocol?

Comments: If there are industry standards, identify them. If not, you should explain your justification for the tests as part of your answer.

Q: Isn't it true that the procedures you followed are not completely relevant to this case?

Comments: Do not bite on the use of the adjective 'completely relevant.' Explain why the procedures you followed were relevant.

Q: Isn't it true, Mr. Expert, that your opinion is based on what you were told by the client, or by the client's employee.

<u>Comments</u>: This suggests that your opinion was not derived from factual investigations, tests or analyses, but simply from secondhand information.

TACTIC: Remember to do your own work. Whenever possible, verify anything told to you by someone else.

> Q: Isn't it true that you did not perform the blood work on the plaintiff?

<u>Comments</u>: If you relied on data from others, as doctors often rely on laboratory results, you must be able to explain your reliance on a third party as being customary in your field.

Questions That Denigrate or Demean

Small openings in your work can lead to large tears in the fabric of your credibility. People in all disciplines make mistakes and oversights. Expert witnesses are no different. If the mistake or oversight is not severe, and does not negate your opinion or conclusion, a single error will not do you in. Nevertheless, a cross examining attorney will attempt to gain extra mileage from any errors on your part. For example, suppose you hear this question:

> Q: Mr. Expert, are you telling the court that you spent months working on this case, and yet completely ignored checking out this important possibility?

You may hear just such a well phrased question, whether you have made an outright error, an oversight in your work, or whether this so-called ' important possibility' is just one possible alternative of many. The attorney is trying to get under your skin with the sarcasm. At the same time, he is suggesting to the jury that you missed an important possibility. He implies that you must not be that good a professional if you missed that possibility, given how much time you spent.

You could become angry at the implication. If it is partly true, you could feel defensive and dismayed that you made an error. Either way, maintain your composure and calmly address all parts of this attacking question. But your first response to this compound question should be a simple "No." When asked to clarify, you might agree that you did spend months on the case but that the so-called possibility was not important. You might further explain that you did not ignore it but had discounted it for the following reasons. If you did ignore it by mistake, you will have to admit that. Hopefully, you could then explain why that omission does not affect the opinion that you offered.

The Hypothetical Question

Your work in the case dealt with real facts and real issues that led to your real opinions. An attorney will sometimes ask how changing one or two relevant facts in the case would change your thinking in the case. His hypothetical question may not even be possible; in that case, state that it is not even a feasible alternative. But the hypothetical question can present a feasible alternative. If you have already considered this alternative, then you probably have an opinion about what the hypothetical changes might mean.

Let me give you an example of how to counter this hypothetical question technique:

Q: Mr. Expert, I'd like you to assume the following fact: no password is required to access Mr. Defendant's computer. I'd also like you to assume the following second fact: the defendant was home sick on the day the computer was used to break into my client's network. Isn't it possible that someone else could have used his computer on that day and that person could be responsible for the electronic break-in?

A: I will make those assumptions, but my own investigation of the defendant's whereabouts and the defendant's computer do not support those facts.

TACTIC: You should differentiate the facts in the case from the suggested facts of any hypothetical question.

A goal of the opposing attorney in offering a hypothetical alternative is to have you enunciate a new opinion that may be different from the one you presented in your report. You have to respond to hypothetical questions but you also have to clarify why any response to a hypothetical differs from your opinions in this case.

If the attorney is sharp, then the hypothetical changes will be subtle enough to confuse jurors, and possibly even confuse you or make you unsure of your original results and opinions.

If the hypothetical question is complex or confusing, do not hesitate to restate it and ask if your restatement is correct. Your restatement of course should be simple, reasonable, and if possible, make any absurdities in the hypothetical question apparent to the jury:

Q: If the defendant only lives 25 miles from his office isn't it possible that he had plenty of time to drive home, murder his wife, and return to his office before his normal lunch hour was over?

A: I want to be sure that I understand your question. Are you asking me whether I believe that it was possible in one hour for the defendant to leave his desk at Noon on the seventh floor of his office building in downtown Los Angeles, walk to his car, drive through downtown LA traffic, cover 50 miles from his office to his home and back again, park his car, walk back to his office, and be back to his desk by 1pm? Is that your question?

Hypothetical questions can be subtle; subtlety on the attorney's part requires acuity on your part. Take your time in answering. Think through the proposed hypothetical question carefully. Identify what differences exist between the hypothetical and the facts in the case that you have analyzed. Identify the differences between the real and the hypothetical situation. Anticipate where the opposing attorney is going, and why the proposed hypothetical situation should not affect your opinions and conclusions.

As long as you can identify and enunciate the differences between the real case and his hypothetical case, then you can simply point those differences out. You can explain why the real facts and the hypothetical proposal do not have the same basis. Be able to explain why the opinions one could draw in the hypothetical situation would naturally be different.

Questions that Try to Anger You

This next question may come after conflicting opinions have been presented:

Q: Considering other testimony that you have heard, Mr. Expert, is it not possible that you may have made a mistake with your opinion?

Here is a poor answer:

A: No, not at all! It's incredible that you would even say that. I've already told you the work I did, all the tests I ran, the results that I've brought here today. I know everything about the science in this case now, and I've been doing this work for nine years.

<u>Observations</u>: it sounds like you became defensive. It sounds like you became angry. It sounds like you became argumentative with an attorney when you should have simply stayed calm and maintained your position. A better answer would have been:

A: I have listened carefully to the other testimony, and I have considered it all. I remain completely convinced, based on my careful investigation, that my original opinion is valid.

At this point in your answer, you have an opportunity to restate your original opinion for the benefit of the jury and for your side in this matter.

Avoiding Absolute Answers

Your expert opinion is supposed to be based on what is most probable, not what absolutely happened.

TACTIC: An expert witness must analyze the possibilities, and conclude what is the most likely explanation.

If you claim that your opinion is absolutely the only one possible, the opposing attorney is likely to ask you a series of questions to which you will have to explain why every single alternative possibility had to be discounted. If you are asked whether you have an opinion, you answer very simply yes or no, and then wait for the follow up. For example:

Q: Mr. Expert, do you have an opinion about why the airplane crashed into a mountainside.

A: Yes, I do.

When asked to explain further, offer your opinion and the basis for that opinion. Be precise and concise. Any answer that goes too far risks damaging your effectiveness.

For example, a bad answer to the above question would be: "The plane crashed because of pilot error. Clearly, since the plane was on autopilot, the pilots had less time to react when they realized how close they were to the mountain. Also, the error in the avionics database misled the pilots about where the plane was in that regional airspace. Finally, the fact that the air traffic controllers spoke English with a foreign accent also caused pilot confusion."

Observations: First, you said too much again, and you made the absolute claim that pilot error was the only reason for the crash. You should have only stated your specific opinion, along with your reasons and basis for why you believe your conclusion to be the most probable explanation for the crash.

It may well be that pilot error is the most probable answer, but why be so absolute? Why eliminate in your phraseology all other possibilities? Why give the other attorney the opportunity to use your extra sentences to suggest to the jury that instrumentation failure, or errors in instructions from air traffic control, or errors in computer data could have contributed to the crash as well as pilot error? Exactly which expert witness are you? Are you a licensed airline pilot who can legitimately comment on the autopilot portion of the plane and related issues like pilot reaction time? Or are you a computer expert who has discovered an error in the avionics database? Have you had any experience speaking to air traffic controllers in foreign languages or in English? Are you qualified to make comments about what may or may not have misled the instrumentation and the software that controls those instruments? Your opinions should stay within your skill set.

Avoiding Guesswork in Your Answers

You should never guess in a deposition or trial setting. You are there to offer your well-founded opinion. Do not be led casually into guessing about other possibilities. A tough questioner will not make it obvious that he is asking you to guess. For example:

Q: Mr. Expert, what do you think could have been done to remedy the complete failure in the hospital's computer systems?

A: Are you asking for my opinion?

Q: I would like to know your thoughts.

A: My opinion is that a well planned training program for hospital employees would probably have avoided the failure.

Observations: the attorney was hoping that you would guess at other possible explanations. You avoided the trap by politely and simply reiterating the opinion you came to give.

Avoiding Legal Determinations

Testimony is not coffee conversation. You may be testifying in an accident case in which someone was hit by a car, and your assignment as an engineer was to measure the skid marks and report to the court. Your opinion has been solicited about the probable speed and direction of the car just before the accident. That is why you are there.

You are not there to offer judgments about whether the driver should have been going more slowly, whether the victim should have looked both ways before stepping into the street, or whether the city should install a stop sign at that particular corner. When you are asked to give a judgment outside the specifics of the area of expertise you were hired for, make sure you recognize that, and act appropriately. For instance:

Q: Mr. Expert, isn't it true that the victim should bear some responsibility for the accident for not having looked both ways before crossing the street?

A: It's not my place to make that judgment here.

Observations: The expert has not fallen prey to the trap of offering a personal opinion or judgment that the opposing attorney can use to affect the jury. If the expert actually offered a personal opinion here, he may have inadvertently been drawing a legal conclusion about contributory negligence, which is not within the expertise of an engineer.

TACTIC: Even if you do not realize an underlying point of law, you must stick to professional opinions and avoid presenting personal ones.

Avoiding the 'Hired Gun' Trap

Remember that you want to be sure not to appear as if you are parroting the opinions your retaining attorney has fed you. For example:

Q: Mr. Expert, did you discuss your testimony before coming into this room today?

A: Yes

Q: With whom did you discuss your testimony?

A: I talked with Mr. Andrews, the defense counsel.

Q: What did he tell you to say?

A: He told me to just truthfully answer the questions.

Q: And did you rehearse your testimony with him?

A: No, but I did review my notes while preparing for my testimony.

Observations: you listened carefully, and you did not fall into the trap of agreeing that you were told to say anything or that you rehearsed some predetermined and scripted set of responses.

Setting up Conflicts with Other Authorities

An interesting gambit used by well schooled attorneys is to find publications that you confirm are authoritative in your field. If you admit that a publication is authoritative, you have given the other attorney the opportunity to quote anything they like from any page within that publication and possibly use it to contrast with one of your opinions. You will then have to explain why your opinion runs counter to what a recognized authority or authoritative journal in your field says. It will not matter that the quoted passage is out of context, or even irrelevant to your case. What will matter is that you have already admitted blindly during testimony that a publication is a reliable authority and to be believed. How should you prepare in advance for this question?

Q: Mr. Expert, I have here a copy of a well known book [or journal]. Isn't it true that experts in your specialty regard this as an authoritative journal?

A: Portions of that book [or journal] are authoritative, but I would have to look carefully at the section in which you may be interested.

From time to time, this gambit may be applied to books or journals in which you have been quoted as an expert in your field. Just because you know that a publication referred to you does not mean you should answer such a question any differently. Do not let your ego guide your response.

TACTIC: Hedge your response about any publication being a reliable authority in all that it might print.

Avoiding Concession Questions

You are not a lawyer, but the opposing lawyer will be perfectly happy to have you weigh in on legal issues that may compromise your side of the case. If you are asked a question that contains anything that sounds like legal terminology, you should be cautious about responding with anything other than a request to explain the terms used. Before testifying, have a discussion with your retaining attorney about the legal issues involved, the legal terminology that governs the issues, and any local jurisdictional standards that may apply to your testimony. This knowledge will be important for you to avoid getting trapped into admissions or concessions because of ignorance of the legal context.

In addition to legal terminology and concessions that you may be tricked into giving, you have to be alert to innocuous sounding agreement questions. In most cases, both attorneys know which facts are not disputed. Often an opposing attorney will state a supposed fact and then ask you to agree with it. For example:

Q: The defendant programmed the system. Isn't that true?

If you know the answers to questions like this, then there is no problem answering. Problems occur when you assume a fact just because the opposing attorney convincingly states it. Any time you are asked whether a statement is true or not, consider that a possible trick. You should be sure of the truth or falsity of a statement before you confirm with your answer that you accept it to be true. You will be more likely to avoid problems like this if you have a discussion before testimony about which facts in the case have been agreed on by both parties.

Summary of Lesson 9

This lesson focused on the most popular types of questions used by attorneys during questioning, both in depositions and at trial. You learned the top Do's and Don'ts for answers to such questions, and a host of pluses and minuses for both how to phrase your responses and how to act during your testimony. You learned how to defuse certain questions, how to repel others, and how to avoid weak responses to the kinds of questions that you can expect to hear.

10

Preparing for Testimony

Legal matters can take an unbelievably long time. Research that you think should only take a day or two can take weeks. Reports that you think should only take a few days to prepare can take weeks. Papers that have to be filed with the courts, and copies that have to be made and sent to experts and other attorneys can take months to create, submit, and review. Getting to the final stage of a trial, or even getting to the point where you can have serious settlement discussions, can take years.

You may have completed your investigation and your expert report years before the day on which you finally present your findings in court. Preparing for testimony before trial requires diligence and attention to detail. Lawyers spend years learning and relearning the best ways to examine and cross-examine witnesses. In these final lessons, I'll introduce some new questioning methods and re-emphasize some important ones from earlier lessons.

Testifying in Mediations, Arbitrations or in Court

You will learn in this lesson how to best prepare to testify in a court of law or as part of a mediation or arbitration. Although the setting and participants will vary somewhat, the overall scope of your preparations should be similar. In each of these settings, you will have done equivalent research and investigations, and you will have reached your conclusions. If you have prepared a formal expert report, you will be subjected to intense scrutiny and questioning about your work and your opinions.

Each of these judicial proceedings will have attorneys on both sides and sometimes experts on both sides. A court of law may appear more formal, and more intimidating, but do not be misled into thinking that mediations and arbitrations are any less important or intense. You must still come to those settings equally well prepared with your opinions, and equally well prepared to handle questioning about your methodologies and your work.

In mediation, one person will have been selected and agreed on by both sides to serve as a mediator. Mediators are often attorneys or retired attorneys who attempt to analyze the facts of the case, interpret the findings of the experts and seek to find reasonable and acceptable common ground for an agreement between the parties. Mediation is the most informal process and often takes place at the mediator's office. No court reporter is there to record everybody's words, and the experts are not usually sworn in under oath. However, each party will still present its case, both experts will have their opportunities to testify, and both attorneys will have their opportunity to cross-examine the experts. In addition, the mediator can choose to pose a variety of clarifying questions to the experts. The mediator's goal is to help resolve the issue by bringing his or her intelligence to evaluate the dispute and to help resolve it.

Arbitration is less formal and less expensive than a trial, although more expensive than mediation. The American Arbitration Association sets the fee schedules for its members. Often, 'binding' arbitration is used, in which both parties agree in advance that the decision reached by the arbitrators regarding an outcome will be accepted. The same questioning and cross examination by attorneys, and additional questions by the arbitrator(s), goes on in this judicial forum. While it has the lesser formality of mediation, binding arbitration incorporates even more finality than a typical courtroom decision. Since the results of arbitration are generally final, it is almost always a less costly approach than going to court and trial. Of course, choosing binding arbitration foregoes the opportunity to present your case to a jury of your peers.

Federal Rule of Evidence 706

One additional appointment that you may receive is that of Court Appointed Expert, sometimes called a special "Master". The appointment is defined by Rule 706 in the Federal Rules of Evidence, and spells out the responsibilities, burdens, and compensation. To save money, both sides in the case will sometimes agree on this individual expert witness to act impartially to review the evidence, to perform the same analyses and investigations and to come to a set of final opinions.

TACTIC: The position of court-appointed expert represents a truly balanced opportunity for an expert to analyze evidence, run tests, perform analyses, conclude opinions, and influence the judicial process.

You will report the results of your work in this setting to a judge who will finalize his ruling based on your objective analysis. This can be more fun than being hired by one side or the other because neither side expects you to tilt your work toward them. Both sides have agreed to pay half of your costs, and you have no other expert trying to counter what you have to say. Since they are trying to save money, you usually do not even have any depositions or cross examinations by attorneys on what you have done. Nevertheless, according to Rule 706, you are still subject to possible depositions that would include questions from both sides, as well as cross examinations by the court and either party to the suit.

I have been retained multiple times as a court-appointed expert. Each time, I did my work, reported my findings, and the judge made his ruling. In each case, the facts that I uncovered were clear, and the attorneys had agreed in advance that there would be no deposition or cross examinations so both cases ended with my reported opinions. However, it is interesting to note that the losing side in these matters usually still disputes the findings and may attempt to hire you afterwards to help them with an appeal or a related follow-on lawsuit. Obviously it would save them effort and cost to have an expert who already knows the facts rather than having to hire a new expert. Nevertheless, it still felt unethical to me to work for one side after being hired by both to help the court in the matter. I also wrestled with the fact that it would have been easy money since I had already done the work to understand the case fully. If you arrive at that point, you can make your own decision.

This role of court-appointed expert only appears after you have been an expert witness for a while and you gain a reputation for thoroughness, professionalism, and objectivity. But you will love it when it happens to you.

The Expert Witness's Role in the Proceedings

In most cases, the attorneys know in advance roughly how many days or weeks have been allotted to the entire case by the judge. In the beginning of each case, the attorney for the plaintiff will present his case. Following the plaintiff's presentation of his case, the defendant's attorney will present the case for the defense. There may be eyewitnesses and there may also be other fact witnesses called to testify. At some point during each of the two halves of the case, the experts will be called to present their findings and opinions.

If the plaintiff hires you, then you will testify during the first half of the trial. If the defense hires you, then you will testify during the second half. Regardless of when you begin your testimony, your retaining attorney will ask you questions first. This first presentation of fact and findings by you is called the 'direct examination.' During direct examination, your attorney asks questions to make your findings known to the court. After you have had this direct opportunity to present the relevant data and opinions that you have to offer, then the other side's attorney will question you. This questioning by the opposing counsel is called the 'cross examination,' and it is a dangerous phase of the trial testimony for the expert witness.

Answering questions under the bright lights at a trial is the ultimate for an expert witness. It represents the culmination of your and everybody else's work. Money, reputation, and sometimes even lives are at stake. The ability to testify successfully at trial is so important that Lesson 11 focuses solely on how to do that. You may spend months or years preparing materials, meeting people, having conversations, performing analyses, and writing reports, and it all leads to this moment. The direct examination by your attorney is largely stress free because you should know in advance the gist of what your attorney will ask and what you intend to say. The questioning by the opposing counsel is the hardest part, and dangerous to the reputation and ultimate value of an expert witness. Lesson 12 focuses solely on performing well during cross examination.

Primary Responsibilities of the Expert

The final preparation phase for a trial includes several well-defined steps:

- Reviewing your notes

- Preparing mentally.

- Rereading and refreshing your memory of key documents, reports, and depositions.

- Reviewing the other expert's work and preparing your attorney with a series of valuable questions that he can ask the opposing expert.

Beyond those steps, you can help by explaining the purpose of any of your questions that may not be self evident to the attorney. And, you can offer suggestions for follow-on questions that your attorney can consider using depending on the answers the other expert gives him to the initial set of questions.

Reviewing Your Own Materials

You should always start by rereading your own expert report. All attorneys involved in the case will question you about its contents.

TACTIC: Reading your own expert report is an excellent way to refresh your memory about what you concluded, and why you came to those conclusions.

Next, open the rest of your file, which should be organized chronologically, and read everything in it. Study your notes about meetings, conversations, tests, results, and discoveries. If your case file contains documents that you considered important at the time, reread them.

Generally, by the time you reach a trial, many depositions have taken place, and you will have taken note of the ones you used to form your opinion. Reread the deposition sections of your expert report to refresh your memory about who said what, how they said it, and in what context they said it.

If you flew around the country or abroad to work on cases, it will not always be practical to revisit locales and relevant sites. If your case is local, however, that may be easy for you to do. Refreshing your memory visually about the location of events can be helpful. If you cannot visit in person, do your best with the photographs you took, recordings you made, and notes you wrote about the site or the people at the site.

It is helpful to create a chart listing the key people involved in the case; you will certainly be asked questions about them and need to know their names and how they fit in the larger scheme of the case. The jurors, judge, and the attorneys will expect you to be familiar with much of what they said, as well as their roles in the case and the opinions you are expressing about them.

Overall, you should be familiar and comfortable with whatever you have committed to paper and included in your case file. Further, the facts and findings that have been discovered by you, or anyone else whose materials you relied on for your final opinions, should be readily available in your mind. By this point, you should be able to give your opinions, present your methods and findings, and answer questions about them without hesitation.

Rereading Other Relevant Case Documents

In your expert report, you explicitly listed everything you reviewed and considered that led to your opinions. Deposition transcripts and relevant other documents that have been Bates stamped, such as emails or letters, are all important to review. Your testimonial answers will be more comprehensive if you carefully reread all appropriate case documents.

If you based your opinion on any official documents, standards, or published industry practices, you should also review those documents and refer to them during your testimony.

For example, most jurisdictions have local civil codes that govern the drilling of a well, or the paving of a road. Companies engaged in interstate commerce may be subject to federal rules and guidelines with specific codes. Doctors, psychotherapists and insurance companies are subject to codes or identifiers that are accepted in their industries and provide a framework for identifying and treating mental illnesses. The DSM, or Diagnostic and Statistical Manual, is the accepted standard. If you are testifying in a medical case, it would be wise for you to review the relevant pages and codes within the most current DSM to refresh your familiarity with the issue in your case.

Refresh your memory about the meaning of common acronyms in your industry.

Benefits of Rereading Your Own Deposition

In preparing for trial, rereading your own deposition is very important. As much as possible, the other attorney will try to trip you up based on answers you gave during your deposition. If you made mistakes, you will hear about it. If you were sloppy in your expressions, you will hear about it.

Conflicting testimony between your deposition and the trial will always represent an opportunity for the opposing attorney to attempt to discredit you, and perhaps legitimately so. Conflicts between current and previous testimony may be enough to warrant that the judge dismiss you and your testimony.

If you neglect to study your own deposition, you will not be as likely to remember exactly what you said. You will not be as likely to state things in the same way during trial as you expressed them during your deposition. You will not necessarily remember the context in which you answered earlier questions. Smart opposing attorneys may quote your own statements during a deposition to present a conflict with new statements you may have just made during a trial. If you have reread your own deposition, you will know the context of any such quotation and can instantly point out the different context, thereby explaining any seeming discrepancy.

If you do your homework and conduct your expert investigation well, and nothing new has been introduced in evidence, then you probably will not have a different opinion at trial.

Benefits of Reading the Other Expert's Deposition

During this final review, reread the other expert's deposition and discuss his opinions with your attorney, even though you will have done this already when you originally went through it. You can reiterate and discuss the specific strengths and weaknesses of the opinions, and develop a joint trial strategy. Knowing what areas to concentrate on during trial to highlight your strengths and the other expert's weaknesses will help your attorney's presentation of the case. It will also help you when you are on the stand. And refreshing your memory about what the other expert said in his deposition will make it easier for you to compare your positions.

The opposing attorney may ask you to validate or confirm a particularly strong opinion of the other expert. If you agree with it, that's fine. If you perceive some flaw or weakness, incorporate that observation into your answer. And if you disagree with the opinions expressed for any reason, you will have the added benefit of a recent rereading to help you discuss the differences between his opinion and yours.

TACTIC: Use post-its when rereading depositions to temporarily mark certain pages that you want to discuss with your retaining attorney, or comment on during the trial.

Revisiting Any Relevant Sites

If in reviewing your notes, recordings, photographs, and other materials you determine that a visit to the actual sites you originally reviewed is essential to your testimony, even if those sites involve considerable time or distance, make that clear to your attorney. Generally, this requires both planning and approval from various people. The sooner you make known such a need, the better will be the chances that you will obtain that site revisit.

If you are representing a defendant or plaintiff who owns or manages the site in question, it will be easy to gain re-access to refresh your memories. But if the other side controls access, they may not grant you an additional site visit. However, if enough time remains before trial, and if any new evidence has been introduced since your previous visit, it becomes more likely that you will be allowed re-access to the site.

Helping your Attorney with Questions

Remember that your attorney wants to slant the other expert's testimony to his advantage, just as the opposing attorney wants to do to you. These lessons will help you to help your attorney perform that more effectively. This starts with you reading everything the other expert has written in the case. His report may contain a rebuttal to what you wrote. He may have signed affidavits or declarations that affirm his support for technical positions in the case. And his deposition will contain valuable information your attorney needs to know.

Analyzing the Other Expert's Deposition

By this point, you have already conveyed to your attorney any errors, oversights, or mistaken assumptions the other expert has made. You can now help phrase questions that your attorney can use to call attention to those mistakes and point out the other expert's technical weaknesses.

Avoid offering advice about the obvious questions for your attorney – he or she will be able to sift through the academic background and occupational experience of the other expert to ask basic questions about them – and save your expertise for defining technically precise questions. For example, if one part of the case requires civil engineering knowledge, but the opposing expert is a mechanical engineer, your questions can highlight the technical differences. This will help your attorney to better demonstrate what may turn out to be a weakness in the other expert's credentials for this particular case.

Credentials and academic background are not necessarily the best place to find weakness in the opposing expert. Look at the technical procedures, industry logic, precise tests, and overall foundation which should support his expert opinions, and determine whether he missed an important technical step or failed to meet an important industry standard. Experts with strong credentials do not always play the expert witness role well. They may fail to do the work that must be done to come to a legally defensible opinion or to express it in a court of law. Not only must an expert opinion be well-founded, well-documented, complete, and accurate, it must be reached by a logical process of steps that are correct, sufficient, and defensible.

The other expert's conclusion or opinion may even be correct, and any one of your colleagues might generally accept it without contention. Part of your responsibility is to discover when the opposing expert does not carry out his expert witnessing role well and does not sufficiently lay a foundation for his opinion(s). Uncover the technical flaw(s) and leave the legal presentations to your retaining attorney.

Being an expert witness is markedly different from simply being an accepted industry guru or an accepted specialist in your own field. Understanding this aspect of testimony will help you to make stronger presentations of your work, and will also help your retaining attorney to ask more effective questions of the other side's expert.

TACTIC: If an opposing expert does not realize that he has done his job poorly, point that out so your attorney is better prepared to question him.

Helping in this way does not make you a biased advocate for your side. It reinforces that you are a team player, ultimately benefitting your client, your attorney and yourself. Your reading of the opponent expert's deposition carefully will help your attorney to prepare a better series of questions, and help you differentiate the other expert's methodology from your own careful and professional approach to your opinions.

Ensuring Your Attorney's Knowledge of the Technical Facts

Remember that your efforts are part of a team effort. You may sometimes feel that you have been hired to perform a technical chore only. That is your minimum responsibility, yes, but it helps to take a broader perspective of your role.

Most attorneys need you to help them understand the technical elements of the case. In earlier lessons, I made it clear that one of your roles is to help educate attorneys about the technical elements of the case. I have also talked about your role in helping to prepare your attorneys for their own questioning of the other side's experts during their depositions. Beyond that, you can help your attorney better understand what the other experts said in their depositions or say in their written reports.

You should review with your attorney the key technical elements that underlie your answers and opinions, and the key strengths and weaknesses of the opposing expert's opinions. You will not be able to help him during the cross examination of the opposing expert so he must understand enough of the technical elements to be able to ask follow-on questions to the other expert's answers.

Do not assume that your attorney understands the technical elements. Take time to review technical points with him so that you are sure he understands. Do this in the context of reviewing important opinions, both yours and the other expert's. Review aloud what you believe to be the key technical facts that you and the other expert plan to present. Review the underlying science, technology, or industry specific issues that underlie those opinions, both yours and the other expert's.

TACTIC: Review with your attorney what you believe to be the strengths and weaknesses of the technical opinions of both sides.

Ask if he understands or wants additional explanations. This teaching role is one that you may have performed at the beginning of the case and continued during the process of discovery and depositions. But you still have a responsibility for ensuring that both you and your attorney are completely prepared for the trial phase.

Designing Demonstrative Evidence

Consider and prepare for how best to explain your opinions to a layman on the jury during your testimony. Conjuring up visual designs and exhibits, usually called "demonstrative exhibits," is your job. These exhibits can take different forms and the choice is up to you primarily, although you should listen closely to your attorney about their effectiveness with the jury. The jurors may use these exhibits in the jury room during their deliberations, so design your exhibits with this in mind. They should be easy to understand, and should convey the precise message you want jurors to understand. Correlating a single exhibit with a single opinion is an excellent strategy. Some ideas for exhibits might be:

- A colorful graph to represent boring and extensive data. Use this technique to summarize a large quantity of data in an easily digestible way. Each graphical summary must be completely accurate. If the graph that you create is new and creative, and meant to be symbolic of a portion of the data, show it to the attorney and others on the team. Ask them if is clear and accurately depicts the data.

- A video of a laboratory model or reconstruction of an event. By showing the court a video of your model or reconstruction, you can better control the conditions, avoiding potential equipment problems in the courtroom.

- Blowups of photographs, maps, or medical films such as x-rays. These are completely factual, well received, and can guide the jury engagingly to the precise visual nature or location of the facts you want to discuss. You can also use an exhibit to highlight a small portion of numeric or textual data from other evidence that has been introduced in printed form.

- Whiteboards, blackboards, or overhead transparencies are low-tech devices on which you can write to make points during a standup presentation.

Your attorneys will probably hire a professional to prepare the exhibits, based on your designs. To be sure they are ready for trial, design the exhibits far enough in advance to review them to ensure they have been created correctly and according to your instructions. Test them to determine if they are readable, pleasing or even exciting to use, and quickly and easily understandable. Additionally, they must be shown to opposing counsel well before the trial.

If time is limited, or if you are not confident that your attorney has personnel to prepare your exhibits, then you should hire your own graphic consultant to prepare the exhibits for you. Remember that the exhibit has to be designed to demonstrate your data, metaphor, or other information. Verify that the final exhibits are accurate and that they are similar to the precise subjects they represent in the litigation

Regardless of who prepares the exhibits, they are yours as long as you oversaw or directed their preparation. Your attorney is ultimately responsible to ensure that they are admissible to the court as evidence. Your attorney should know the legalities, such as obtaining a stipulation from the opposing counsel or a court order approving them for use during the trial.

Work with the attorney. Between you, make sure that your demonstrative exhibits meet this criterion.

TACTIC: Review any exhibit concepts with your attorney in advance, before money has been spent, to

make sure that each exhibit contains the proper foundation for your use during testimony.

Final Reviews and Rehearsal

If you have attended to the subjects of this lesson, then you and your attorney should both be ready. You have reviewed the technical elements in the case. You have refreshed your memory about everything you have written and thought about the case. You have refreshed your attorney's memory or clarified his understanding of the technical elements of the case so he can better cross examine the other expert. You have discussed the likely questions that he is going to ask you during direct examination, and you can prepare for the best possible answers. You have also discussed the likely attacks on you and your opinions that may come from the other side, and you have discussed the best ways to respond to those attacks.

From time to time, you will be involved in large or complex cases, and you may be one of several experts hired to testify to different elements of the case. It will be important to discuss the scope of each expert's testimony with the other experts on your side, and your attorney or attorneys. Although each person's testimony will usually be specialized, they may overlap in technical content. You want to be clear about who is testifying about which subjects, and everybody's testimony needs to be consistent in terms of the overall presentation of the case. Often, opposing attorneys will ask similar questions of multiple experts to impeach or undermine other experts because of contradictions in what they may say.

Your preparations should also have included the writing of a set of principal questions for your attorney's use during your direct examination. In all likelihood, he will merge some questions and replace others with questions of his own choosing. In any event, you will have ensured that everything you can think of regarding the science and foundation of your opinions is brought out during questioning. In addition, this final review should include your writing of a series of suggested questions dealing with the technical elements of the other expert's opinions. These should include any questions that might address the other expert's uncertainty or weakness, or that bear on his methodology, logic, or final opinions.

Practicing for a Deposition

Finally, you should give thought to the ways in which you will express your answers to your attorney's direct examination questions and the questions that may come during cross examination. Run through a simple rehearsal with your attorney in which you verbalize answers to all expected questions to get his thoughts on what you have to say. Even if your attorney doesn't fully understand the technology or science behind your answers, it will still be instructive to get his feedback about your choice of words, down to your use of adjectives. You may be surprised at how incisive his suggestions can be when it comes to how the opposing attorney might treat your use of seemingly simple and innocuous phraseology. Preparation in a practice session does not mean that you have to memorize anything – you should already know the details of the case and the content of your own investigation.

If your deposition is going to be videotaped, practice with your attorney on video. This will enable you to identify any annoying unconscious physical mannerisms. They are easily eliminated. Your attorney will be able to review your answers with you and coach you directly on the reasons why particular phraseology or delivery of answers is wrong, ineffective, or worse still, harmful to his legal case.

Additional suggestions regarding videotaped depositions: Dress conservatively and avoid flashy jewelry. Avoid excessively long pauses, and avoid eating or drinking while being videotaped.

TACTIC: To prevent your speech from being drowned out by electronic noise, avoid touching the microphone.

In cases where your testimony may go on for more than a day, or when considerable amounts of money are involved, many attorneys advise that you participate in a 'mock trial.' This is a live exercise with you and two attorneys, probably from the law firm that hired you. Usually, your attorney will practice the direct examination questions with you, and the other attorney will practice the cross examination questions. This allows your attorney to object as necessary, and allows you to become more comfortable with your own retaining attorney.

If you are not experienced, this process will introduce you to the sorts of questions you may be asked, allow you to recognize the style of questioning to which you may be subjected during the real trial, and give you an opportunity to develop a sense of assuredness and calmness in responding to questions, which will help you to maintain your composure. Finally, this will give your attorneys valuable feedback about your answers and the delivery of them.

Ask your attorney for his coaching help after the mock trial. Find out from him which answers can be improved, and make sure you understand why. Learn what trap questions you may hear, and ask for suggestions about the best way to circumvent or avoid them. My experience will help guide you around the general boulders in your path, but your attorney's experience will guide you around the specific obstacles to success in his and your specific case.

Summary of Lesson 10

Final preparations for testimony were the main object of this lesson. I emphasized the importance of reviewing, rereading, and revisiting specific materials, sites, and other evidence before testimony. In particular, I explained the benefits of careful review of deposition transcripts and other documents written by you and the other side's expert.

I also explained ways in which you can help your retaining attorney to better prepare for questioning you and the other expert. I offered advice on developing demonstrative exhibits that will help you to present your information and further influence the jurors. Lastly, I explained how your review of the facts and the law with your attorney can greatly enhance your final testimonial result during both direct and cross examination.

11

Testifying Successfully

Testifying in court is challenging; it can be intimidating to the inexperienced, and can go from rewarding to frustrating to embarrassing in the span of three sentences. Even for an experienced witness it can be daunting and fatiguing.

As you hone your skills you become more and more valuable, beyond simply the knowledge you bring to the case. This knowledge, presented well, can make the difference between settling and not settling, between going to trial or not.

That is the key: presenting incontrovertible facts, and presenting them professionally despite the tactics and ploys of the opposing attorney.

Your Role in Court

The lawyers in a case have their shot at convincing the jury in a variety of ways and usually over several days. You have just one shot. Remember that it does not matter if you think you are right. You have to convince the jury in the limited minutes or hours of your testimony that they should believe what you have to say. You need to present your facts, and present them well.

TACTIC: In court, your facts should be correct, but it is equally important that you sound and look convincing.

Leading up to Your Testimony

The preceding lesson discussed the many preparations that you must make in the days or weeks that lead up to trial testimony. Let me share with you some things that you should think about in the twenty four hours preceding your testimony.

Traveling by airplane on the day before trial testimony can be stressful – flights get canceled, delays happen. If you are an out-of-town expert, you should consider traveling one to two days before trial testimony so that you arrive early and are calm by the time of trial.

TACTIC: Schedule a pre-trial conference with the attorney on the day before trial. Do your travelling either that morning or the preceding day.

You can use the day before trial to review important materials. You can also schedule a pretrial meeting with your retaining attorney. Getting a good night's sleep is always beneficial the night before a trial. Some people suggest that you do not drink any alcohol the night before trial, but you should know yourself well enough to make that decision. If you are taking any prescription medicine, discuss that with your attorney, since it might have an effect on your energy level during the trial day. The attorney can adjust the order in which he calls witnesses to call you at your best time.

As I suggested earlier in the discussions about deposition testimony, do not take anything to the witness box that you do not explicitly need for your testimony. If you feel that you need your entire file folder with you for reference, you should ask your attorney to review it to make sure that nothing of a privileged nature remains in it.

Remember that dressing conservatively conveys professionalism. Comb your hair, and make sure that your clothing is clean and freshly pressed. When on the stand, restrict unnecessary movement. Do not look fidgety, if possible. Eliminate any frequent tics, if possible. And finally, sit up straight. No slouching, no hunching. Your personal bearing can have an incredibly positive effect on the sense that everyone in the courtroom, especially jurors, will have of you as a credible, professional, and authoritative witness.

TACTIC: if you carry any papers or your file folder to the witness stand, carry them in your left hand. When you raise your right hand to take the oath, you will not have to switch hands, taking the chance of dropping any of the documents.

Characteristics of your Testimony

Jurors expect that experts come to testify with opinions that support the side that hired them. Otherwise, why would they be testifying? However, they still need to be convinced that you truly believe the claims you are making. You have the important job of convincing the jury that you joined the case to investigate independently and evaluate the facts, that you performed tests of your own choosing, and that you eventually reached the supportable and defensible positions you are presenting.

First, jurors have to be convinced that you deserve their confidence. You must have the experience, knowledge, or credentials necessary to do what you say you have done. Second, they need to believe that you fully understand the elements of the case and have taken the necessary and appropriate steps and followed industry accepted methods. In short, you need to exude confidence that you have done these things, that you understand them, and that altogether, they led to your opinions.

People do not like to listen to boring witnesses. This has nothing to do with competence or qualifications; it has everything to do with effectiveness in court. A great expert witness, like a great teacher, sounds natural when he speaks, and appears personable and likable. He chooses words that are easy to understand, along with explanations that use interesting analogies or examples. He entertains with his voice and with any demonstrative exhibits he has created.

TACTIC: As an expert witness, be honest about what you do not know, and confident about what you do know.

Ideally, you want to have a human side that will make the jurors think back to a favorite teacher. A good way to do this is to sound warm and enthusiastic about what you are presenting.

The bottom line is that your job is to persuade your listeners that your opinions and conclusions are the right or the better ones. Some jurors will already have an opinion about the case by the time you testify. Others will have no opinion. In both cases, you will have to persuade those jurors that your opinions are correct. Logic and facts presented by you will rarely be enough. Effective persuasion is essential. No small chore.

Making an Entrance

"Call the witness!"

Yes, that is you. And it is your time to shine or fade. Going into court is a combination of many things. It is partly a first date, partly a conversation with your boss, and partly a public speech.

You will have butterflies as an expert witness. But if you enjoy center stage, you will get over them in moments.

Your audience – the jury, most importantly – wonders what you have to say, and how well you will say it; in the first seconds after you walk in the door, most of the people in the room are forming judgments about you.

Conveying Professionalism and Confidence

They wonder if you are worth the money you are being paid. They wonder who dressed you that morning. They wonder about your hairstyle. You do not need to spend $400 on a Hollywood hairstylist, but you do need a haircut.

TACTIC: Beyond your appearance, the jurors wonder if you can make heads or tails out of what they have heard so far in the case.

If they haven't yet judged the contents of the case, they wonder whether you will be able to explain it to them any better than the previous witnesses and attorneys.

They wonder what your manner of walking says about you. Are you strutting down the aisle to the witness box? *Overconfident, cocky*. Are you shuffling down the aisle to the witness box? *Uncertain, unbelievable*. Are you walking briskly but confidently? *All business, sure of himself. Okay, let's hear what he has to say.*

Establish and Maintain Credibility

All those impressions form before you open your mouth to say your first word. The moment you begin to speak, everyone hears your voice, they see your posture in the witness box, they note how pleasantly or confidently you look at the attorneys, the judge, and the jurors. They observe whether you avert your gaze by shyly looking down at your papers or at the floor. They judge in advance and without justification whether they should believe what you have to say, before you have even said it.

It's show time.

The Main Phases of Trial Testimony

After you have been sworn in, your hiring attorney will start with questions designed to show your qualifications, and to present opinion testimony. This is the 'voir dire' phase. The term 'voir dire' comes from the French and roughly means "to speak the truth." In the United States, voir dire applies twice during a trial. The first time occurs during juror selection. Prospective jurors are questioned about their backgrounds and any potential biases to determine which of them will be chosen for the jury. Voir dire also occurs when expert witnesses are questioned about their backgrounds and qualifications to determine their admissibility for offering expert opinions.

First will be the easy questions from your retaining attorney about your name, your current and past employment, and your education. You will also answer questions about any additional training you received in your specialty, memberships in any professional organizations, and any special credentials or certifications you may have. The opposing attorney may ask questions in this phase in an attempt to clarify parts of your background and experience. He may attempt immediately to discredit or disqualify you, or simply lay a legal foundation for questions to be asked later.

The second main phase of trial testimony is the direct examination in which you will be asked familiar questions by your retaining attorney about your opinions and your investigations. His series of questions will enable you to recount how and when you joined the case, what work you performed, what factual findings were determined as a result of your analyses and efforts, and what your expert opinions are about those findings. The attorney will ask you to explain to the court the foundations for those opinions, largely drawing on your specific methodologies, any known industry standards or guidelines, and any peer reviews that were performed on your work.

The third phase of trial testimony is the cross examination. The opposing attorney has the opportunity to ask you questions about any of the facts in evidence you have reviewed, and about any of your responses to questions during direct examination.

Cross examination can be damaging, demeaning, and frustrating. The cross examining attorney may attempt:

1. To discredit you personally for your conduct, or for your limited experience and knowledge in the specific subjects covered by the trial.

2. To discredit you professionally for your choice of tests, for the scope of your analyses, for the extent of your investigation. His questions will try to make it seem as if you didn't do enough, or you didn't do it right, or you didn't even do the right things.

3. To discredit your final opinions. This can come in a host of ways. He may try to convince the jury that your conclusions do not logically, completely, or accurately lead from the set of facts that you considered. He may try to confuse you to make you seem less knowledgeable or competent than you are. He may point out errors in your data or propose other conclusions that could have or should have been drawn.

A fourth phase may occur. 'Re-direct examination' occurs after the opposing attorney has cross-examined you. If your retaining attorney feels that the cross examination damaged you in a repairable way, or misled the jury about your testimony, he can ask a series of additional questions. Your attorney may only ask questions about subjects that were broached by the opposing attorney during cross examination. Both his intention and yours will be to minimize the importance of any points made by the cross examining attorney, and to give you a final opportunity to restate your main opinion. This will generally be short, if it even occurs. Act and answer as confidently as you did earlier in the trial.

Another phase may still occur. If your attorney has asked any questions in the re-direct phase, then the cross examining attorney will be able to ask additional questions. This final phase is called "re-cross-examination." Each of these phases is short because the rules limit the attorneys to questions only on subjects broached in the preceding phase. During re-cross examination, the opposing attorney can only ask questions about what your attorney brought up during re-direct. Nevertheless, you need to maintain your alertness just as you did throughout the cross examination phase.

Keeping Their Attention

Let's back up a bit and remember that you have center stage when you are testifying. You have the attention of everyone in that room, and while you answer questions, the superficial judgments will continue. The jurors will judge your demeanor, your presence, and your comportment, as well as the content of your words. Your voice is paramount. Deliver your answers in a confident, steady way, while enunciating clearly and loudly enough to be heard by anybody in the room.

When you are in the witness box, everyone in the jury box needs to hear you. Be aware of your voice level when you are in the witness box or at your demonstrative exhibits. If you write or draw on some form of display board, you should write both legibly and large. Also, try to not turn your back on the jurors. If you must, stop talking briefly while you write.

Avoid Being Boring

In this setting, you can be a storyteller. During direct examination, in which you present your opinions and the bases for them, you can use gradual changes in volume or pitch to tell your story. However, if voice control is not your forte, you will have to pay attention to sudden changes in the volume or pitch at which you are speaking. Naturally, you do not want to be boring, so ...don't ...speak ...in ...a ...fixed ...rate ...monotone. You may laugh now, but in the serious setting of a courtroom, you may fall into patterns of speech that might not be normal to you. Just use your intelligence and remember:

TACTIC: Use natural speech that is not monotonous, has no sudden changes in volume or pitch, and is loud enough so people can hear you.

General Techniques for Answering Questions

No matter how long a trial is, many participants are anxious for it to end. The jurors want to go home for obvious reasons, the attorneys and clients have had their fill of it as well, and the experts just want to testify, go home, and get past the pressure. Often, the judge imposes deadlines on the attorneys for the duration of the trial as a whole and the testimonial time of the witnesses.

Trial testimony could be as little as 15 minutes or as much as an hour or two. Do not be misled into thinking that trial testimony will take anywhere near as much time as did your deposition.

TACTIC: Listen. Listen. Listen … to the question. If you do not hear the question fully, or if you do not understand the question completely, how can you answer it effectively and correctly?

My advice about answering questions still applies. Understanding and following that advice is even more urgent now. Your answers have to be on target. You must answer the question directly and only the precise question that is asked. If you answer each question with as short a reply as possible, it helps to protect you and to move the proceedings along. In addition, the jurors will more likely be able to follow your answer. Shorter sentences are easier to understand, and help the jurors to more easily stay connected to your line of thought.

Stick to Simple English

Remember that you are not talking to colleagues or to students in a graduate class. You are talking to a group of random people, some of whom may not have even gone to high school. Sentences with simple words are best. Your answers should not contain acronyms and special terminology from your discipline. If you do use them, take a moment to explain it to the jurors. Opposing attorneys sometimes purposely use these technical terms because they want you to lose the jurors' attention. When an attorney uses an acronym or other technical term in a question, do not just respond by answering his question with the term in it. Take a moment before answering the question to explain the term to the jury. Then, you can go ahead and answer the rest of the question. Remember simple English. Remember that you want to keep the jurors attentive to you.

TACTIC: *If you have to look over a document at the request of an attorney, do not talk while you are looking at it. When you are ready to talk again, look up from the document and look over at the jurors.*

In my experience, jurors stay attentive when I use simple metaphors, simple analogies, simple examples, and simple visual exhibits. I emphasize the adjective simple here, because you can always explain complicated things in simple ways. Do not make the mistake of thinking that your science, technology, or special discipline requires a complex explanation.

Students in a classroom may ask you detailed questions that require technically precise explanations. In the judicial setting, people just want to understand. They just want to "get the idea." In this situation, simplicity means clarity. If you can convey the essence of an opinion to the other people in the room with a simple word or analogy, you have done your job. You will have kept their attention, and you will have explained it well enough to have been convincing.

Connecting With the Jury

When somebody asks you a question, you typically look at that person when you answer. A trial experience is different. Although an attorney asks you a question, direct your response to the jurors. You have to act as if a juror had just asked you the question. To be polite and to look semi-normal, you have to pay attention and look at the attorney while he's asking you the question. When the question is over, however, you can turn toward the jurors and begin your response. Looking at the jurors will be a new experience; it is counterintuitive, and may feel odd to you when you do it. But it is an important part of keeping their attention.

Because the first questions your attorney asks you will generally have to do with your qualifications, and the judge determines whether you have the qualifications to be accepted as an expert in your field, you could address the judge with your answer. If that is feasible, go ahead and do it. I find that in most trial settings, the witness stand faces out in the same direction as the judge, and is usually set on a lower platform. Attempting to crane my neck or body to look at the judge is uncomfortable so I strike a balance by varying between looking back at the attorney, looking over at the jury, and looking up at the judge.

In general, one or two jurors will listen closely and understand what you are saying. Make eye contact with them and allow their gestures and their body language to encourage you in your explanations. You will have a sense of whether the jury understands, accepts, and is convinced by what you are saying.

If you see by their facial expressions or head gestures that they do not understand your answer, then the earlier advice regarding short answers will not apply. Keep their attention by rephrasing your answer with a new analogy or in a different way — but still as simply as possible. Long answers are still a bad idea, even if you believe you have been asked to elaborate on something. Limit any elaboration to several sentences. Anything longer and you may bore the jury.

During cross examination, an opposing attorney may try to cut you off because he does not want you to be any clearer to the jury or to make points with them.

TACTIC: If you believe that you need to say more as part of your answer, you can say aloud that you have not finished your answer yet and you need to do that.

The lawyers may argue among themselves at this point, but more often than not, you will be allowed to continue to answer and explain. The positive part of this is that the fracas between the attorneys will capture the juror's attention and keep it on you during any continued response. The side benefit is that those jurors with whom you were directly making eye contact will be the most likely ones to be able to explain this part of the case to other jurors during subsequent deliberations. So your efforts will bear fruit later and have value beyond the few moments of your response. When your answer to an attorney's question is complete, you can shift your gaze back from the jury box to the attorney to await your next question.

Testimony by Video Conferencing or Telephone

The age of computers, teleconferencing, and the Internet brings another possibility to your testimonial arsenal. You may under certain circumstances testify by phone or video conference. This can happen if you are ill and cannot attend the trial, but are still able to testify at a distance. You might also be stranded in a distant city because of weather or transportation difficulties, yet still be able and willing to testify. Finally, you may actually volunteer (or be asked) to testify from your own office, in order to save the litigant money. Occasionally, clients of limited means may require or readily accept this alternative form of testimony.

In general, this alternate form of testimony is less desirable for all concerned for a number of reasons. First, it loses the personal aspect of testimony, in which you can see the reactions of the judge, jury, and attorneys, and adjust your testimony in a variety of ways. Second, these same participants cannot see you directly, and it becomes more difficult to control the 'stage'. The best advice to remember is to look directly and earnestly at the very center of the camera, if you are using video. This is the closest you will come, in effect, to eye contact with the triers of fact in a trial.

On the other hand, some attorneys believe that being willing to testimony in this less personal way will create good will with the attorney. This may in turn generate additional expert witness work in the future. Also, it reduces your travel time, which reduces wear and tear on you, especially in these transportation-challenged times.

Words to the Wise

You will be especially pleased when you can see that jurors agree with what you are saying. Some basics:

- Keep your answers short. Attorneys learn to be brief so as not to lose the jurors. That is good advice for you as an expert witness for the same reason.

- Be precise in your responses. "Yes" Or "No" is better than "Probably." Fifty-three miles an hour is better than "about the speed limit." Precise answers sound knowledgeable while imprecise answers sound uncertain.

- Use everyday English, not technical jargon or big words. Attorneys do not use legalese when asking you questions, once again to avoid losing the jurors. You should do the same; lose the jargon, not the jurors.

- Be a teacher. Take a moment to define or explain any technical words you have to use. Just don't come across as arrogant while you are doing it. Use simple English.

- Be crystal clear about each opinion. Each one of your opinions is like the main course at a fancy restaurant. A waiter tells you the name of the course, then describes what ingredients were used and how the dish was prepared. The jurors want to know your opinion, but they also want to know the ingredients (the facts and information) you used, and then hear about the careful, methodical, and logical way in which you prepared that 'dish' for them.

- Rephrase an answer if the jurors appear confused. Also rephrase an answer if your attorney, during direct examination, seems to repeat a question. It may be because he believes your answer was confusing or because your answer did not include important facts that he wanted to hear from you. A repeated question by your retaining attorney is an indication that your preceding answer was not enough. Elaborate or clarify.

Maintaining Your Composure

Maintaining a calm composure is an excellent way to stay centered and focused. It helps to enhance your credibility during direct examination, and to protect that same credibility during cross examination. Losing your composure on the stand, under any manner of attack from the opposing counsel, is unprofessional, and plays directly into opposing counsel's hands.

In a trial setting, opposing counsel hopes that the jurors will recoil from you in one way or another, maybe based on how you look or sound or due to questions they might have about your credibility. One sure way to make them doubt you is by losing your composure, for any reason.

Attempting to drive a wedge between you and the jurors is something the cross examining attorney could very well attempt. If he can upset, anger, or visibly distress you, you are a giant step closer to losing control. If you become angry, you are more likely to make mistakes, either outright ones or simply verbal opportunities for additional attacks by the opposing counsel that will successfully undermine your testimony. If you become defensive, the jurors will wonder how confident you really are of what you have to say. Worse, the opposing attorney may successfully make you wonder, at this last minute, whether you might have been wrong in one of your assumptions, procedures, or opinions.

The trial is not the time for uncertainty. New evidence is rarely introduced at trial time, so you likely know all you need to know before you enter the witness box. If something completely new is introduced, you will sound flexible and reasonable if you are willing to consider it, but you should say that you would have to make a full review of the new information before concluding whether it would justify changing your opinion.

If you are sure of your opinions, and confident in your work, you should be able to present those opinions straightforwardly and without uncertainty. In the face of challenges from the opposing attorney, you should be able to maintain that certainty and confidence in what you say.

TACTIC: Always act calmly on the witness stand. Always seem to be in control. Always answer clearly and thoughtfully.

Being Honest and Unbiased

When I say, "be honest," it should be obvious that I mean at least "speak the truth." But I mean something even more than that: I am also saying: "Don't stretch the truth." You may believe strongly in the client and in your side of the case, but remember that you are not supposed to be biased. You are not supposed to be an advocate for your side. You are supposed to be an expert who presents evidence helpful to that side, but in an objective manner. You risk being disqualified, or impeached, by the judge if it becomes obvious that you are stretching the truth and drawing conclusions that go beyond an unbiased, expert appraisal of the evidence.

Helping and Not Hurting Your Side during the Case

Discussing assumptions that you've made, preparing demonstrative exhibits, and comporting yourself in the courthouse environment are all ways to both help and avoid hurting your side.

Discussing Assumptions You Made

Discuss any assumptions you made during your work, with your retaining attorney in advance of trial, and be prepared for a series of questions during the trial that address those assumptions.

Your attorney may directly ask you about each assumption you made, why you made it, and ask you to explain exactly what trade-offs you considered. These questions and your answers can defuse the effects of similar questions from the cross examining attorney. During the direct examination, you will be allowed the time and opportunity to give helpful answers. For example, you might explain at that point your decision to choose criteria that were sensible to you, as well as why you made those choices or assumptions. Perhaps, in your opinion, those assumptions had the greatest support in your scientific literature, or because the assumptions were consistent with the general methodologies used in your industry.

Cross examining attorneys may also ask you questions about assumptions you made. Their intent may be to show that your assumptions were mistaken but more commonly they will try to introduce doubt with the suggestion that a small change in an assumption might have led to a different opinion or conclusion. If the cross examining attorney asks you questions about assumptions, he may lead the questioning to reduce confidence in your opinions.

Using Demonstrative Exhibits

In the preceding lesson, you learned about preparing demonstrative exhibits. During a trial, there are ways to make more effective use of those exhibits. Remember that demonstrative exhibits are different from the attachments to your expert report. An exhibit of this nature is generally much larger so the jurors can easily view it. Think about creating one exhibit for each major opinion that you offer to the jury. Do not clutter it with excessive graphical or textual or numeric information. It demonstrates the essence of your opinion in a few seconds -- hence the name 'demonstrative exhibit.'

In a trial, a picture is unquestionably worth a thousand words because so much more rests on your ability to explain the facts. Exhibits of a visual nature become more and more beneficial when the issues and your specialty are more scientific or complicated. Some people learn better from pictures than words or numbers. Deliver expert witness testimony in both visual and verbal ways so the jurors who learn either way will understand you. Eye-catching, colorful, and easily understood visual aids will complement the greater detail of your text, tables or spreadsheets.

Realize that the jurors may look at your exhibits on their own, well after you have presented them. The meaning of your exhibits should be evident to the jurors when they look back at them. This suggests that you should design your exhibits so that they can be easily looked at afterwards.

TACTIC: Do not rely on live demonstrative exhibits during courtroom testimony.

You might be tempted to create a flashy, three-dimensional, moving exhibit that reconstructs events for the jurors. Unfortunately, though, you just never know when machinery or materiel in the courtroom may not work. Create your exhibit in advance, make a video copy, and introduce the video as your demonstrative exhibit. The jury can easily review such a video, whereas they would not be able to reconstruct a live demonstration.

Here is your opportunity to be a great teacher. When you present demonstrative exhibits you have an opportunity to be active, often to leave the witness box, to have your voice express your enthusiasm, and to be physically more engaging to the jury. Let your enthusiasm and excitement for the subject matter, your exhibits, and your results just spill over from you to the jurors. Don't overact, but realize the opportunity for some acting.

Have your demonstrative exhibits covered until you are ready to use them. If they are visible to the jurors before you are ready to discuss them, they will distract the jurors from your testimony. On the other hand, leave them uncovered after you use them during direct testimony. They will continue to affect the jury by being visible. Also, you will be able to refer to them during cross examination if you wish. A skilled cross examiner will not let you go back to your demonstrative exhibits during his cross examination. It will be to your benefit if you have 'neglected' to cover them up and if he has neglected to remove them from the jury's view.

Being Professional outside the Courtroom

This entire lesson has focused on acting professionally and effectively inside the courtroom. An error that some expert witnesses make is to forget that they must maintain their professionalism outside the courtroom as well. The court will take breaks, and you may find yourself in the hallways, in the bathroom, in the cafeteria, or in neighboring restaurants. Anyone within earshot may be a juror, a member of the opposing legal team, or a member of the court.

Be alert and be discreet in what you might say about the case, the client, the strategies, or any of the other people and players in it.

Even when you are careful about what you say and where you say it, you will still be at risk. For example, if you are social and you start conversations with people at the water fountain or in the hallway, one of those people you chat with could be a juror. A conversation with a juror is an error that could cause a mistrial. It is safer to simply not start conversations with anybody you do not know in a courthouse. If someone starts a conversation with you, you can certainly be polite, but keep the conversation short and limited to sports or the weather, not the trial.

Another possibility in a major case is that a member of the press corps might try to interview you, either before or after you testify. Once again, you are safest if you make no comment. A polite response might be to offer your business card, but not to answer questions.

Summary of Lesson 11

Your preparations for trial can be distilled down into three key roles. The first role is that of investigator, in which you study the case, seek out additional facts, and perform necessary tasks. Your second role is that of teacher. Since the facts are specific to your field of expertise, you have the responsibility to educate the jurors in non-technical ways about what those facts mean. Finally, your third role is that of analyst: the opinions you present represent your analysis of the technical facts about the issues in the case.

The aim is to establish your credibility and persuade the jury to your point of view. You follow proper methodologies to obtain technical information, and then explain the technical results, and finally you persuade the jury that your results and opinions are the most logical and ultimately believable.

In this lesson, we discussed the various parts of your role in court during your testimony, from capturing to keeping the jurors' or judge's attention. I explained the main phases of trial testimony and gave general guidelines for answering questions. I offered several ways to connect positively with the jury, to explain assumptions, and to create and use demonstrative exhibits. Finally, we covered issues important for maintaining your professional conduct in the courthouse when you are not testifying.

12

Minimizing the Dangers of Cross-Examination

Cross examination by the opposing counsel is the most dangerous time during your testimony. This is when you will feel the most pressure, because you know that the opposing attorney may challenge your credentials, will try to undermine your opinions, will explore whether you have made any conflicting statements, and will make various efforts to cause you to lose your composure. The attorney may smile but his goal is to destroy your credibility with the jury, the judge, the arbitrator or mediator, and everyone else within earshot.

You have control over many things before trial that will lessen your vulnerability to cross examination. Your CV should accurately reflect everything you have done in your career, and you should be comfortable and familiar with everything in that CV. Only take on cases that are within your sphere of expertise. Any time you venture an opinion or comment about something beyond your strengths, you risk credibility with the jury. Lawyers know how to latch on to misstatements, poorly chosen words, and especially statements that go beyond your documented skills, experience, and knowledge.

When you reach the stage of cross examination in a trial, you have already gone through direct examination. You and your attorney have had a chance to present the entirety of your work efforts. Your investigations, tests, and analyses should have been thorough and methodical. If you present those facts well during direct examination, you will establish a much more difficult starting position for the opposing attorney during cross examination.

TACTIC: What you do know, answer confidently. What you do not know, admit readily.

Your responses need to be clear and concise, direct and precise, objective and fair. If you agree with a question, feel free to say so. If you disagree with a cross-examiner's statement, you can also say so, but you should prepare to explain fully the reasons for your disagreement. Between those extremes of agreement and disagreement, you should prepare to qualify any question that attempts to slant the truth toward the other side.

The Best Guidelines to Follow

Later in this lesson, I will explain both subtle and advanced responses that you can use, especially as you become more experienced at testimony. However, regardless of whether you are a beginning or experienced expert witness, let me share with you some simple guidelines.

- You can answer most cross examination questions with a simple statement of fact. Alternatively, you can respond with the following simple expressions: "yes," "no," "I don't know," "I don't recall," and "I did not understand your question."

- Never ramble on in your answers. Only provide in your answer what the question requests.

- Never answer questions with phrases that express uncertainty or that begin with, "I guess," "I believe," "I presume," or "I think." Do not hedge your opinions in court the way you might at a party or in coffee conversation with friends. Your expertise and your science should enable you to draw conclusions and present opinions that are correct to a reasonable degree of medical or scientific certainty, based on the technical evidence and your work. Answers that begin with technically weak phraseology will not meet the legal burdens of proof required in a court of law.

TACTIC: Leave some leeway when relating a series of events, or a list of facts. Do not simply say "that's everything"; instead, say something like "that's all I recall right now."

- Allow the attorney to finish his question completely. Also wait for one to two seconds before answering. In addition to providing your attorney with an opportunity to object to or comment on the question, this will give you a bit of time to think about the question and your best answer.

- Finally, avoid sounding arrogant or condescending, or making jokes or light hearted remarks. Your words can be too easily turned around by attorneys.

Cross Examination Attacks on You

Let's talk about the weaponry given to attorneys in law school for treating expert witnesses during cross examination. Some of these techniques may not apply to you, or even to your sphere of expertise, but they are common approaches used by lawyers. Give them some thought and prepare to handle questions based on these approaches.

The opposing attorney may ask you any number of the following types of questions, and not in any particular order. The best way to defend against probable attacks during cross examination is to become familiar with the most common forms, and to understand the examining attorney's goals. Having answers to those expected questions will reduce your stress and minimize the likelihood of falling prey to well-known cross examination methods.

Using Your Prior Work against You

Attorneys with an inclination toward thoroughness and preparedness will do their homework before questioning you. They will discover things about you and your previous work, as well as any testimonial efforts, in several ways. Note the following items to prepare for the types of strategies a methodical opposing attorney might take:

- He may ask his own expert what he or she knows about you in your mutual specialty.

- He may speak to attorneys who worked with or against you in previous cases.

- He may assign support staff, or hire graduate students in your field, to learn of any weaknesses you may have. To do so, they may:

    o   Obtain copies of advertising you use to promote your services.

    o   Search publications in your specialty for quotations from you, or your colleagues at the same company or school where you work.

o   Find and review your previous writings and testimony. You should realize that even though Rule 26 requires you to disclose publications in the last 10 years and testimony in the last four years, attorneys are not constrained to asking you questions solely within those years. If their research finds that you have previous publications or previous testimony, they may ask you questions about anything they find in those previous writings and testimony.

o   Look for contradictory public remarks on issues similar to this case that may have appeared in the body of any speeches or seminars that you may have delivered or even have scheduled for delivery.

o   Use a search engine to find websites that reference your name. Then, they will look for any discrepancies between credentials listed there and your CV.

- Finally, attorneys will probably learn the names of existing peer-reviewed publications in your field. Be aware of the existence of these peer-reviewed publications as well as what they say about your methodologies.

TACTIC: In an effort to use Daubert criteria to challenge the admissibility of your testimony, attorneys look for relevant articles that discuss the methodology you have used.

You cannot rely on incomplete or evasive answers about your own methodologies as compared to the authoritative ones discussed in peer reviewed publications. Knowing about the existence of such articles will help you anticipate questions during cross examination. In addition, if you have done this research before you even reach the investigation and reporting phase, you will have made your earlier work even more solid.

Attacking Your Qualifications and Testimony

First, opposing attorneys might attack your qualifications and credentials. Perhaps your degrees were not directly relevant to the case or you did not even complete a degree program. Maybe your experience in the industry was not on target. Are your experience or degrees out of date? What have you done recently that is directly related to the specific case about which you are opining? Are there time gaps in your professional work experience? What were you doing during those gaps? Are there any discrepancies between your CV and the credentials listed on your business website or your university's website?

Prepare reasonable answers to any questions you can think of about your qualifications and credentials. Assume that the opposing side will see or discover opportunities for attack here. Don't ignore any weakness in your qualifications and credentials. Discuss such a weakness in advance with your retaining attorney. He may well want to consider addressing the weakness in some fashion to minimize it during direct testimony.

Next, you will almost always be attacked for some form of bias. Perhaps you always work for the defense, or always work for the plaintiff. Have you worked often for this particular law firm that hired you? Perhaps you have written something that expresses a clear-cut advocacy for a cause that may be connected to this case. Have you recently written something silly but relevant and now public on your Facebook, Linkedin, or Twitter account? Think ahead to what possible opportunities may exist for attempting to convince the jury that your testimony is slanted. Prepare answers to those efforts that may paint you as a biased expert.

Attacking Your Investigation

Next, attorneys will attempt to call into question the factual basis of your entire investigation. They may claim that your facts were inadequate, and even seek your support by asking questions that suggest other steps that you may have missed or other procedures that you may have chosen not to include. Stay confident of your work, but prepare to answer questions that suggest inadequacy. Be prepared to explain what things you chose not to do and why. Also be prepared to express confidently why the scope of your work was enough to lead you to your conclusions.

TACTIC: Remember that you do not need absolute conclusions. You only need to express your best opinion, based on the most probable scenario and to a reasonable degree of scientific or medical certainty.

Good cross examiners have a set of effective questions that attack the adequacy of expert witness investigations. When asked during cross examination, it will be devastating if any of them hits home and can demonstrate either oversights or weaknesses in your work effort. I discussed several of these types of questions in Lesson 9. If you do not recall those, you can review them in the section of Lesson 9 entitled "questions meant to attack the factual basis of your testimony."

You may fall prey to such questions because your attorney or his client told you it was unnecessary to do so-and-so or that they did not want to spend the money for you to do such-and-such. You might not have been permitted to run additional tests. You might not have been allowed to complete certain site reviews. You might not have been authorized to create reconstructions of certain events.

You may have the best intentions but from time to time, you may be subjected to limitations that restrict what you can do or say. You will have to discuss that with your attorney. You may need to prepare explanations. You might dismiss the omission as unimportant, or as something that you chose not to do because it was not necessary. If any of those activities that you did not do were necessary, then you may no longer be able to express the opinion you expressed.

Using 'Learned Treatises' to Uncover Contradictions

Attorneys will also look for apparent contradictions between your testimony and statements that may appear in textbooks that are authoritative in your expertise. The attorneys may use journal publications that are respected and professional, as well as published articles by other recognized experts in your field. This approach to undermining your testimony is called the 'learned treatise' technique. This technique relies first on establishing a published work as a 'reliable authority.' If that is done by your admission, then any relevant portions of that work can be read into the record as substantive and contradicting evidence.

Two things could constitute your own 'admission.' You may admit during questioning that the publication is a reliable authority. Or, you may have quoted from or referred in your earlier testimony to a passage from the publication. Either of these mean that other sections from this 'authoritative text' can potentially be used to contradict your testimony or support the opposing expert's testimony. Either way, you need to be up-to-date on your readings of learned treatises in your field. You should have done your own research before trial to see what others may have written about the subject in which you are testifying.

TACTIC: You should almost always refuse to validate any other expert or publication as authoritative in your field!

If the opposing attorney asks you to confirm for him that a particular author, publication, book, or other expert, is an authority in your field, only say "Yes" if you know everything ever written or spoken by that authority. Otherwise, hedge your answer with an honest statement of usefulness of the publication, or unfamiliarity with the particular work or expert.

Ironically, you may be the very expert whose writings are quoted to undermine your own opinion in the case. If you have written articles or books that speak to the same subject as the current case, be aware of any earlier statements in writing that contradict current statements or positions you are taking. If discrepancies or contradictions appear, you should have an explanation prepared for those differences.

The same is true if you have testified in any earlier cases in which your deposition or trial testimony is a matter of public record. You will have to explain any previous statements that may run counter to current opinions, if they are discovered and brought up to you during the trial. You ought to know if this is possible, and you should have some good answers ready. As a valid explanation, for example, the facts referred to in a previous publication could be different from the facts in this particular case. Also, the state of knowledge in your discipline may have expanded since the previous publication. Current opinions may now run contrary to earlier industry opinions because of this new and greater knowledge.

Your Field of Expertise May Be Unrecognized

Your particular field may be new. Both relevance and reliability are part of Daubert considerations that are used to determine whether your proffered testimony and opinions will be admitted into evidence. Computer forensics was not even a field with a name in 1990. DNA analysis was not a recognized field of expertise in the mid twentieth century. In both cases, both fields developed recognition and credibility over a period of years.

If you testify in a trial in such a field, you can help assure the admissibility of your own testimony. Come to court with information about any growing recognition of your professional field and any learned treatises that others may have written that substantiate the viability of the field itself. Doing research about other court cases that may have used experts in your field would help, as well. Using the Internet for such research is a perfect example of a field of expertise that did not even exist a few decades ago.

If your field does not have an obtainable academic degree, professional associations, or certifications, you still can bring in your particular experience and expertise to offer opinions and present testimony. However, this particular attack is one that you should carefully discuss with your own attorney. To take the wind out of the cross examining attorney's sails, your attorney may well want to address this particular weakness in advance during direct testimony.

An additional ploy used to attack your particular field of expertise is to quote well-known writers whose theses or science may be out of date. Lawyers call this the 'historic hysteric gambit.' Attacks on your particular sphere of scientific expertise can come from quotations taken from Galileo's writings, or references to unsubstantiated 21st century researchers. Your best defense in both cases is to know the history of your profession as well as the current state of its research.

Defending Yourself

I will talk shortly about additional types of questions that you will hear during cross examination. Before those specific examples, I would like to introduce some general approaches to use in responding to all questions.

Be Honest

Honest, careful analysis of the evidence, has led you to honest conclusions. Your opinions are the cornerstone of your testimony, and they should be easy to state. While you are presenting your opinions, you can support them with references to particular exhibits. Reinforce and clarify your opinions with demonstrative exhibits such as graphs, photographs or models. Do not stretch the truth; your opinions should be based on unbiased appraisal of the evidence.

Avoid Speculation

Do not speculate if you do not know the answer. The opposing attorney may ask a range of questions about your professional discipline, the answers to which you do not know. You cannot guess at answers, and you should not try.

TACTIC: People realize that nobody knows everything, even experts. If you do not know an answer, simply say so, which is both acceptable and a good response.

The opposing attorney has nowhere else to go at this point. You may hear some short lived bluster or expression of incredulity that may make you uncomfortable or even embarrassed because you do not know something. But an "I don't know" answer minimizes the bloodletting. You've simply given him no erroneous answer that he can shred, further calling into question your lack of expertise.

Handling Surprise Information

At times an opposing counsel will surprise you with completely new information. Take extra time to assess exactly what has been introduced before expressing your response. This will give your attorney an opportunity to object to the information if that is appropriate. Otherwise, if you have never seen the new material and are not familiar with it, you should maintain your objectivity and fairness, and appear perfectly willing to consider it. In any event, you should state that you have not had any previous opportunity to evaluate the material.

Remember that it should require a startling new discovery to warrant changing your opinions. If the new information presented is relevant to your opinions, you can certainly say that you are willing to consider the information. If you cannot immediately perform the necessary analysis while you are on the stand, say so. If you know immediately that the new information would not change your opinion, say so and explain why, given your expertise and knowledge, this new information can be discounted.

The most dangerous position would be if the new information presented might change your opinion. Be extremely reluctant to change your opinion on the stand. If the new information is totally incontrovertible and presented as factual, you will not be able to do much. On the other hand, hedge your answer if the information presented is only a supposition (remember, listen carefully to the phraseology). Similarly, hedge your answer if the new information is someone else's research that you have not had a chance to review. Short of truly incontrovertible new evidence, you need to maintain your consistency and stick to your expressed opinions.

Retain Control

Cross examining attorneys attempt to maintain control by asking you questions that often lead you down their chosen path. While yes or no responses can often protect you, sometimes a simple yes or no answer is insufficient. At those times, you will need to convey more information to the jury.

One way to keep control is to avoid beginning an answer with "yes, but..." The cross examining attorney (and sometimes even the judge) can easily cut your answer off the instant he hears the word "but." Technically, you have answered the question with the word "yes," and he can legitimately say 'thank you' and move on to the next question.

TACTIC: When your "yes" answer needs clarification, put your qualifying clause at the beginning of the sentence.

For example:

Q: Isn't it true that if the burglar alarm had been set to ON, then no one could've walked through the front door without setting off the alarm?

A: If power to the system had not been interrupted, and if the alarm circuitry had not malfunctioned, then 'Yes.'

Dealing with Mischaracterization of Your Responses

One reason that brevity is so important during testimony is that lawyers learn a wide range of verbal skills. They learn how to phrase questions carefully, and they learn ways to deconstruct a witness's choice of language. Every additional sentence you include in your answer is a new opportunity for the skilled attorney to attack you. So is every additional clause with which you dress up that sentence and every extra adjective or metaphor that you use to more colorfully describe a situation.

Remember that a main goal of cross examination is to reduce your credibility with the jury; to do this, attorneys may attempt to make you seem defensive or uncertain, they may highlight contradictions between your approach and other approaches in peer-reviewed journals, they may try to upset or anger you, and/or may make you defend or explain the individual words or phrases in an otherwise solid technological response.

For example, suppose you have just offered this answer to a question about a test you ran:

A: The failure of the engine I was testing occurred after four hours, and it was preceded by a whining, almost screeching, sound, a bit like fingernails on a blackboard.

You may hear a wide range of questions: Whining, can you explain that? Screeching, could you clarify that? Fingernails on a blackboard, could you describe that more clearly? Please explain the differences among those three. How would those different sounds have suggested a different type of internal engine failure? Isn't it true that different sounds that precede an engine failure could suggest different causes for the failure?

In your colorful answer, you talked way too much. You gave the attorney too many targets. This would have been enough:

A: The failure of the engine I was testing occurred after four hours.

But even a simpler answer does not always stop a skilled cross-examiner. A word in your discipline may have particular meaning for you when used in a particular context. From time to time, an attorney will attempt to redefine or recast the meaning of a word you used in seemingly reasonable alternative ways for the jury. When that happens, you must respond by clarifying the correct use of the word. For example, psychotherapists have different diagnoses for different forms of abuse, such as substance abuse, drug abuse, physical abuse, mental abuse, and so on. An attorney may use the word to mean something else entirely. Your response should be something like:

A: You are now using the word 'abuse' in a completely different way than a professional psychotherapist would use it.

Then, of course, you would explain or restate the correct interpretation and meaning in the context of this particular case.

References to Alleged Misconduct in Your Past

It can be front page news when someone is accused of a crime, but only back page news if the accusation is later retracted. Although not necessarily common, an incident in an expert witness's past can be dredged up to impugn the witness's character. For example:

Q: Are you possibly the Robert Smith who was accused of robbing a convenience store in Portland, Maine, six years ago?

If indeed you were in Portland six years ago, yet the charges were retracted, do not answer with a simple "yes." Your character has been diminished, and the rest of your testimony may be diminished. A better and more proactive answer would be:

A: Although I was accused, the charges were completely erroneous, and they were dropped the following day with an apology from the District Attorney's Office for any harm done to me or my professional reputation because of that unwarranted charge.

More lawsuits take place In the United States than anywhere else in the world. Some of these lawsuits are unfounded, and yet they take considerable time and energy to defend. If any such taint currently lingers in your life, and is brought up during questioning, you will need to address it directly and even indignantly. Rather than shrinking from the charge, as if it had truth to it, simply dismiss it with a straightforward explanation of why you believe the charge had no merit.

Recognizing the Most Common Questioning Traps

You will be able to stay calm more easily if you have spent time anticipating possible questions. You should have done this during those preparatory conferences with your attorney before trial. However, you should still remain alert during questioning to figure out where any line of questions is leading.

Some questions are designed to make you feel incompetent or unprofessional. Other questions are intended to suggest that you overlooked certain professional steps.

Remember that you are the expert, and the attorney may misstate the facts. This could be inadvertent, because he is an attorney and not an expert in your specialty. But it could also be purposeful, because he is trying to trap you into a quick agreement with a statement that is only partially true. Cross examiners have an arsenal of well-known trap questions.

Questions that Challenge You

Questions that begin with "isn't it true that..." are generally challenging in one way or another. The question may end with a statement that is partially believable or true. The tone of voice may be calm or sarcastic, and the question may be presented with a smile, a smirk, or a frown on the attorney's face. Ignore the attorney's facial expression; it is only meant to unsettle you. Treat all questions alike. Stay calm in the face of any question. Listen carefully to every word. Pause briefly before answering, and take longer to respond if the question demands extra thought on your part.

TACTIC: Take your time before you respond to challenging questions. Use the time to analyze each

question, to form a careful response, and to assess where the question is leading.

'Out-of-Context' Questions

As you know, your expert report lists the documents and information that you reviewed. Some of it is information that may have found its way into your analyses and opinions while other content may have seemed inconsequential at the time. You may have read that material more lightly.

It will not matter in court whether you read it in depth or scanned it lightly. If your expert report says that you read it, then the opposing attorney can legitimately ask you any questions he likes about it. You may need to refresh your memory about a document or previous testimony that an attorney references in a question. Be aware that he may be using the information out of context.

When asked a question that quotes from another document, especially if you have said that you previously read it, you should request to see the document at that moment in the trial. Ask for the specific page that contains the quotation, and then take your time finding the place in the referenced document.

Before saying that you have found the place with the quotation, casually look at the context of the discussion that leads just before and follows just after the referenced quotation. If you read the document and roughly remember what it was addressing, this quick scan of context will be enough for you to identify the contextual meaning of the quotation. If possible, think through the reason for the question and why the quotation was given to you out of context. You have to understand how the attorney wants to use this out of context question to help his side of the case.

If a quotation were straightforward, the opposing attorney could use his own expert to agree with it. If it can be interpreted in different ways, his attempt to use the quotation in an out-of-context way is an attempt to use you to help him. Generally, when you look at the context of such a question, look for conditions that were applied in the text around the quotation. Only if those conditions are true would the quotation be valid. You must find or understand the constraints, then point out to the jury why they are different from the facts in this case.

This out-of-context trap can also occur when an attorney reads a passage from one of your own books or articles or even transcripts from a previous deposition of yours. Always ask to see the document or book from which any quotation is taken.

TACTIC: If you are asked a question about something in a document, ask to see the document again at that moment in the trial.

Pigeonholing Questions

A cross examining attorney will sometimes try to simplify your analysis or characterize some of the elements of your investigations. They may ask you to rate something from 1 to 10, or A to F. For example,

Q: "Using a standard grading scale of A through F, how would you rate the hospital's maintenance of their coronary care monitoring equipment?"

If the issue were as simple as 1 to 10, or A through F, you would not be testifying in a lawsuit. You should resist efforts to pigeonhole your answers to accord with any artificial simplification proposed by a cross examining attorney. For example, you might respond:

A: I believe that the issues in this case are complex enough that it would be a disservice to the court to try to oversimplify them into a single number or letter.

Questions about Things You Did Not Do

As another example, let's say you are a doctor and are testifying about a diagnosis for an ill patient. Suppose you directed that a series of blood tests should be run. Perhaps, one of those blood tests gave you the answer you needed about the illness and that guided your subsequent treatment of the patient. Nevertheless, the patient eventually died and you have been sued. Under cross examination, the attorney asks why you did not run a PET scan or why you did not run an MRI on this patient. You are the expert. Is your first response to wonder whether those tests should have been run just because the attorney asked about them?

You should know why you did not run them and what those reasons were. You are the expert. This is a ploy by a cross examining attorney. Do not feel bad, and do not look like you feel self-critical. Take a breath and just explain why you chose not to run any additional or different test. Exude confidence in your methodology and the tests you did choose. Sound calm and comfortable, and show that this question has not shown a weakness in your professionalism. Your answer should simply focus on what you did do and why it became the primary basis of your professional decision.

Fair but Harmful Questions

Though you know you are supposed to be objective and truthful, you may not want to admit a fact that will hurt your 'side.' You may be tempted to hedge your answer or to give an evasive answer.

Forget that thought. If you know about it, and you are being asked about it, then everybody knows about it already except the jury. And they are soon going to learn about it.

TACTIC: Do not take away from your professionalism with an evasive answer. Just admit the fact and be done with it.

Silent Questions

By this point, you should understand that giving more of an answer than was asked is ineffective and wrong. A skilled questioner can use an interesting psychological trick without saying a word. Think about the times when you are chatting with someone or when you are just the speaker in a small group of friends. If you finish what you are saying, and nobody says anything, you are often tempted to continue speaking. An attorney wants you to do the same thing if he seems to pause expectantly, perhaps with a quizzical look on his face.

Perhaps the questioner thinks there should be more to the response. Perhaps he simply did not get what he wants... yet. Perhaps there is more that could be said on the subject. But if you have completed your answer to a question to your satisfaction, you can stop. It is not your responsibility to guess where the questioner would like to go. Just wait. It is the questioner's job to ask questions, but if you have answered the last question and no new question is pending, the proverbial ball is in the questioner's court.

The questioner may even break the silence by asking a simple, encouraging question: "Is that it?" That could have several meanings, but for each of them, the best answer is simply "Yes."

Isn't Your Opinion Just an Opinion?

At some point, the cross examiner will have asked the obvious questions. You will have successfully deflected what you could, and minimized what you could not. But you have not been excused from the witness box yet. One favorite and usually final question attempts to get you to downgrade the strength of your own testimony. The suggestion is that your opinion is no better than the opinion of anybody else who might happen to be in the courtroom at that moment. For example:

Q: So, Mr. Expert, considering these different points of views and opinions, isn't your opinion just an opinion?

Of course it is, you might be thinking, and my earlier statements about simple 'yes-no' answers might tempt you to respond with a "yes." However, a better answer, especially if it permits you to have the last word on the stand, is:

A: Not really; it is my considered professional opinion, based on my methodologies, analyses, tests, and investigations, as well as my review of documentation and materials in this case.

Avoiding Weakness and Uncertainty in Your Responses

You are supposed to do a professional job. You are supposed to follow well-established methodologies. You are supposed to take appropriate notes of interviews or site visits. When you are answering questions about what you did or what you remember, you should be able to answer factually. For example:

Q: Mr. Expert, how do you know that the Defendant was the programmer of the system in question here?

A good answer might simply be:

A: He told me.

A bad answer might be:

A: I'm pretty sure I asked him. At least that's what my notes say.

You should have reviewed your notes and your entire case file before you came into the trial to give testimony. How can you be only 'pretty sure' if that is what you really did? Do you think that answer will boost the confidence of the jury for your other answers? Additionally, why would you quote your own notes? Do you need to refer to your notes on something that simple? If you asked the defendant that question, why are you not confident enough to say that is what you did?

Summary of Lesson 12

Having the 'last word' is just about my 'last word' in these lessons. I have taught you a range of guidelines to follow during cross examination, and I have given you a series of techniques with which to build credibility with the jury. I have explained a host of things that a cross examiner tries to do to you, and offered many techniques you can use to defend against each of these approaches. I have demonstrated sample question and answer sequences that will serve you well as a skillful expert witness during the most challenging portion of litigation – the cross examination.

Appendix A

Glossary of Legal Terms

ACCREDITATION: The process by which competency and authority are established.

AFFIDAVIT: A written statement made under oath.

AMERICAN BOARD OF CRIMINALISTS: A group of national and regional organizations that certify forensic examiners in a variety of criminal related disciplines.

ANSWER: In a civil case, the defendant's written response to the plaintiff's complaint. It must be filed within a specified period of time, and it either admits to or (more typically) denies the factual or legal basis for liability.

APPEAL: A request to a supervisory court, which is usually composed of a panel of judges, to overturn the legal ruling of a lower court.

APPELLATE COURT: A court that reconsiders legal decisions made by lower courts.

ARBITRATION: A method of alternative dispute resolution in which the disputing parties agree to abide by the decision of an arbitrator.

ARRAIGNMENT: The initial appearance before a judge in a criminal case. At an arraignment, the charges against the defendant are read, a lawyer is appointed if the defendant cannot afford one, and the defendant's plea is entered.

ASSIGNMENT: The transfer of legal rights, such as the time left on a lease, from one person to another.

ASSUMPTION OF RISK: A defense raised in personal injury lawsuits. It asserts that the plaintiff knew that a particular activity was dangerous and thus bears all responsibility for any injury that resulted.

ATTORNEY WORK PRODUCT: All preparatory documents and notes of an attorney who is preparing for a trial, all of which become privileged and not obtainable through the discovery process.

BAD FAITH: Dishonesty or fraud in a transaction, such as entering into an agreement with no intention of ever living up to its terms. Also, it could include knowingly misrepresenting the quality of something being bought or sold.

BAIL: The money a defendant pays as a guarantee that he or she will show up in court at a later date. For most serious crimes, a judge sets bail during the arraignment.

BAIL SCHEDULE: The list that sets the amount of bail a defendant is required to pay based on what the charge is. A judge may be able to reduce the amount.

BANKRUPTCY: Insolvency; a process governed by federal law to help when people cannot or will not pay their debts.

BATES STAMP (or Number): Unique identification number/letters that are printed on each page of any document introduced into evidence.

BENCH: Synonym for the judge, as well as where he sits in a courtroom.

BENCH TRIAL: Also called court trial. A trial held before a judge and without a jury.

BENEFICIARY: Person named in a will or insurance policy to receive money or property; person who receives benefits from a trust.

BEYOND A REASONABLE DOUBT: The highest level of proof required to obtain a guilty verdict in criminal cases.

BIFURCATION: Splitting a trial into two parts: a liability phase and a penalty phase. In some cases, a new jury may be impaneled to deliberate for the penalty phase.

BOOKING: Part of the process of being arrested in which the details of who a person is and why he or she was arrested are recorded into the police records.

BRIEF: A written document that outlines a party's legal arguments.

BURDEN OF PROOF: The duty of a party in a lawsuit to persuade the judge or the jury that enough facts exist to prove the allegations of the case.

CASE LAW: Also known as *common law*. The law created by judges when deciding individual disputes or cases.

CAVEAT EMPTOR: Latin for "buyer beware." This rule generally applies to all sales between individuals. It gives the buyer full responsibility for determining the quality of the goods in question. The seller generally has no duty to offer warranties or to disclose defects in the goods.

CERTIFIED REFERENCE MATERIAL (CRM): Any evidence that has been tested for validity by an authorized certifying agency.

CHAPTER 7 BANKRUPTCY: A type of bankruptcy in which a person's assets are liquidated (collected and sold) and the proceeds are distributed to the creditors.

CHAPTER 13 BANKRUPTCY: A type of bankruptcy in which a person keeps his assets and pays creditors according to an approved plan.

CHALLENGE FOR CAUSE: Asking that a potential juror be rejected if it is revealed that for some reason he or she is unable or unwilling to set aside preconceptions and pay attention only to the evidence.

CHANGE OF VENUE: A change in the location of a trial, usually granted to avoid prejudice against one of the parties.

CIRCUIT COURT: Mid level appellate courts, sometimes called the U.S. courts of appeals that adjudicate appeals from district courts within their federal judicial circuit.

CIRCUMSTANTIAL EVIDENCE: Indirect evidence that implies something occurred but doesn't directly prove it. For example: if a man accused of embezzling money from his company had made several big-ticket purchases in cash around the time of the alleged embezzlement, that fact would constitute circumstantial evidence that he had stolen the money.

CIVIL LAW: All legal rules that do not apply to criminal activities.

CLASS ACTION SUIT: A lawsuit in which one or more parties files a complaint on behalf of themselves and all other people who are "similarly situated" (suffering from the same problem). Often used when a large number of people have comparable claims.

CLEAR AND CONVINCING EVIDENCE: The level of proof sometimes required in a civil case for the plaintiff to prevail. This level is more than a "preponderance of the evidence" but less than "beyond a reasonable doubt".

COLLATERAL: An asset that a borrower agrees to give up if he or she fails to repay a loan.

COMMON LAW: Also known as *case law*. The law created by judges when deciding individual disputes or cases.

COMPLAINT: In a civil action, the document that initiates a lawsuit. The complaint outlines the alleged facts of the case and the basis for which a legal remedy is sought. In a criminal action, a complaint is the preliminary charge filed by the complaining party, usually with the police or a court.

CONFLICT OF INTEREST: Refers to a situation when someone, such as a lawyer or public official, has competing professional or personal obligation, or personal or financial interests, that would make it difficult to fulfill his duties fairly.

CONTEMPT OF COURT: An action that interferes with a judge's ability to administer justice or that insults the dignity of the court. Disrespectful comments to the judge or a failure to heed a judge's orders could be considered contempt of court. A person found in contempt of court can face financial sanctions and, in some cases, jail time.

CONTINGENCY FEE: Also called a 'contingent fee,' this is a fee arrangement in which the lawyer is paid out of any damages that are awarded. Typically, the lawyer gets between one-fourth and one-third. If no damages are awarded, there is no fee.

CONTRACT: An agreement between two or more parties in which an offer is made and accepted, and each party benefits. The agreement can be formal, informal, written, oral or just plain understood. Some contracts are required to be in writing in order to be enforced.

CREDIBILITY: The degree of believability of any witness.

CREDITOR: A person (or institution) to whom money is owed.

CRIMINAL LAW: All rules applied against crimes that constitute a significant public concern and are enforced by State and Federal Government against transgressors.

CROSS EXAMINATION: The questioning of an opposing party's witness about matters brought up during direct examination.

CURRICULUM VITAE: A summary document that contains a professional's educational and occupational background.

DAMAGES: The financial compensation awarded to someone who suffered an injury or was harmed by someone else's wrongful act.

DEBTOR: Person who owes money.

DECISION: The judgment rendered by a court after a consideration of the facts and legal issues before it.

DEFAMATION: The publication of a statement that injures a person's reputation. Libel and slander are defamation.

DEFAULT: The failure to fulfill a legal obligation, such as neglecting to pay back a loan on schedule.

DEFAULT JUDGMENT: A ruling entered against a defendant who fails to answer a summons in a lawsuit.

DEFENDANT: In criminal cases, the person accused of the crime. In civil cases, the person or organization who is being sued.

DEMONSTRATIVE EVIDENCE: Any visual evidence, such as graphs, models, or videos, used to demonstrate or make verbal testimony easier to understand.

DEPOSITION: Part of the pre-trial discovery (fact-finding) process in which a witness testifies under oath. A deposition is held out of court with no judge present, but the answers often can be used as evidence in the trial.

DIRECT EVIDENCE: Evidence that stands on its own to prove an alleged fact, such as testimony of a witness who says she saw a defendant pointing a gun at a victim during a robbery.

DIRECT EXAMINATION: The initial questioning of a witness by the party that called the witness.

DIRECTED VERDICT: A verdict ordered by the judge, usually based on some point of law and replacing the jury's role of decision maker. See *Motion for Directed Verdict* below.

DISCOVERY: Part of the pre-trial litigation process during which each party requests relevant information and documents from the other side in an attempt to "discover" pertinent facts.

DISMISSAL WITH PREJUDICE: When a case is dismissed for good reason and the plaintiff is barred from bringing an action on the same claim.

DISMISSAL WITHOUT PREJUDICE: When a case is dismissed but the plaintiff is allowed to bring a new suit on the same claim.

DOUBLE JEOPARDY: Being tried twice for the same offense.

DUE PROCESS: The idea that laws and legal proceedings must be fair and follow reasonable procedures. The Constitution guarantees that the government cannot take away a person's basic rights to "life, liberty or property, without due process of law." Courts have issued numerous rulings about what this means in particular cases.

DUTY TO WARN: The legal obligation to warn people of a danger. Typically, manufacturers of hazardous products have a duty to warn customers of a product's potential dangers and to advise users of any precautions they should take.

EN BANC: French for "by the full court." When all the members of an appellate court hear an argument, they are sitting en banc.

ETHICS: The accepted code of actions, including the concept of right and wrong, of a society or group of people.

EVIDENCE: The various things presented in court to prove an alleged fact. These can include testimony, documents, photographs, maps, and video.

EXCLUSION OF WITNESSES: Judicial rule that bars witnesses from the courtroom except when they testify.

EX PARTE: Latin that means "by or for one party." Refers to situations in which only one party (and not the adversary) appears before a judge. Such meetings are often forbidden.

EXPERT OPINION: An expression of belief regarding what may have occurred, based on the witness's training, knowledge, experience, or education.

EXPERT TESTIMONY: Verbal presentation of evidence and testimony in any scientific or specialized field during a trial, mediation, or arbitration.

EXPERT WITNESS: A witness with a specialized knowledge of a subject who is allowed to discuss an event in court even though he or she was not present. For example, an arson expert could testify about the probable cause of a suspicious fire.

EXPERTISE: Advanced knowledge or skills in a specialized field.

FACT WITNESS: Any person who has first-hand knowledge of events, based on personal observations using the five senses.

FEDERAL RULES OF CIVIL PROCEDURE (FRCP): Body of rules that govern civil trials in U.S. courts.

FEDERAL RULES OF EVIDENCE (FRE): Body of rules that govern criminal trials in U.S. courts.

FELONY: Serious crime punishable by incarceration for a year or more. Such crimes include rape, murder, robbery, burglary, and arson.

FIDUCIARY DUTY: An obligation to act in the best interest of another party. For instance, a corporation's board member has a fiduciary duty to the shareholders, a trustee has a fiduciary duty to the trust's beneficiaries, and an attorney has a fiduciary duty to a client.

FOUNDATION: The entirety of facts, tests, and analyses that form the basis of expert witness testimony and opinions.

FRYE rule: An older rule of court that requires expert witness testimony to be based on reasonable acceptance by the expert's peer community of the technical procedures used to reach the opinions offered.

GOOD FAITH: Honestly and without deception. An agreement might be declared invalid if one of the parties entered with the intention of defrauding the other.

GRAND JURY: A group of citizens convened in a criminal case to consider the prosecutor's evidence and determine whether probable cause exists to prosecute a suspect for a felony.

HEARING: A judicial gathering at which the parties to a legal action present competing evidence and testimony about their positions.

HEARSAY: Secondhand information that a witness only heard about from someone else and did not see or hear himself. Hearsay is not typically admitted in court because it is not considered trustworthy, though there are many exceptions.

HEIRS: Persons who are entitled by law to inherit the property of the deceased if there is no will specifying how it's divided.

HISTORIC HYSTERIC GAMBIT: A cross examination technique in which the attorney belittles the validity of testimony based on science that is out-of-date or too new to be substantive.

HUNG JURY: A jury that is unable to reach a verdict.

HYPOTHETICAL QUESTION: A cross examination question to an expert witness that asks for a new opinion about a theoretical variation in the facts.

IMPEACHMENT: A cross examination process in which the attorney successfully attacks and undermines the credibility of the witness or the validity of the witness' methodologies.

IN CAMERA: Latin for "in chambers." Refers to a hearing or document inspection that occurs privately, such as in a judge's chambers.

INDICTMENT: A formal accusation of a felony, issued by a grand jury after considering evidence presented by a prosecutor.

INFORMATION: A formal accusation of a crime, issued by a prosecutor. This is an alternative to an indictment.

INFORMED CONSENT: Except in the case of an emergency, a doctor must obtain a patient's agreement (informed consent) to any course of treatment. Doctors are required to tell the patient anything that would substantially affect the patient's decision. Such information typically includes the nature and purpose of the treatment, its risks and consequences, and alternative courses of treatment.

INFRINGEMENT: Unauthorized use, typically of a patent or copyright.

INTERLOCUTORY ORDER: Temporary order issued during the course of litigation, used to provide a temporary or provisional decision on an issue. Typically cannot be appealed because it is not final.

INTERNATIONAL STANDARDS ORGANIZATION (ISO): An international group that creates and maintains standards for industrial processes and commercial activities.

INTERROGATORIES: Requests for further information in a civil case. Part of the pre-trial discovery (fact-finding) process in which one side in a case provides written answers to written questions under oath. The answers often can be used as evidence in the trial.

INTESTATE: To die without a will.

IRREVOCABLE LIVING TRUST: A trust created during the maker's lifetime that does not allow the maker to change it.

JUDGE: The official who hears legal cases, oversees procedures, and makes final decisions in a court.

JUDGMENT: A court's official decision on the matters before it.

JUDGMENT NON OBSTANTE VEREDICTO: Known also as a judgment notwithstanding the verdict. This refers to a decision by a trial judge to rule in favor of a losing party, even though the jury's verdict was in favor of the other side. Usually done when the facts or law do not support the jury's verdict.

JURISDICTION: A court's authority to rule on the questions of law at issue in a dispute, typically determined by geographic location and type of case.

JURY: A group of people who render verdicts on legal disputes, based on the facts and evidence presented, and who also may set penalties for those convicted.

JURY CHARGE: The judge's instructions to the jurors on the law that applies in a case and definitions of the relevant legal concepts. These instructions may be complex and are often pivotal in a jury's discussions.

JUST CAUSE: A legitimate reason. Often used in the employment context to refer to the reasons why someone was fired.

JUSTICE OF THE PEACE: An officer of the court who presides over minor infractions such as traffic violations and misdemeanors.

LAWYER: An attorney who represents one party to a dispute in the legal resolution process.

LAY WITNESS: A witness to facts known directly to the witness.

LIABILITY: Any legal responsibility, duty, or obligation.

LEARNED TREATISE: A book or other written publication that is considered both reliable and authoritative in a particular field.

LIBEL: Defamatory (false and injurious) written statements or materials, including movies or photographs.

LIEN: A claim against someone's property. A lien is instituted in order to secure payment from the property owner in the event that the property is sold. A mortgage is a common lien.

LIMITED LIABILITY COMPANY (LLC): A business structure that is a hybrid of a partnership and a corporation. Its owners are shielded from personal liability and all profits and losses pass directly to the owners without taxation of the entity itself.

LIQUIDATED DAMAGES: This is the amount of money specified in a contract that is to be awarded in the event that an agreement is violated.

MALPRACTICE: Improper or negligent behavior by a professional, such as a doctor or a lawyer. This may also include the failure of a professional to follow the accepted standards of practice of his or her profession.

MANDATORY SENTENCE: A criminal sentence set by a legislature that establishes the minimum length of prison time for specified crimes and thus limits the amount of discretion a judge has when sentencing a defendant.

MEDIATION: A method of alternative dispute resolution in which a neutral third party helps to resolve a dispute. The mediator does not have the power to impose a decision on the parties. If a satisfactory resolution cannot be reached, the parties can pursue a lawsuit.

MIRANDA WARNING: The statement recited to individuals taken into police custody. It warns of their right to remain silent and to have an attorney.

MISDEMEANOR: Crime that is punishable by less than one year in jail, such as minor theft and simple assault that does not result in substantial bodily injury.

MISTRIAL: A cancellation of a trial prior to the rendering of a verdict.

MOTION: A request asking a judge to issue a ruling or order on a legal matter.

MOTION FOR A NEW TRIAL: Request in which a losing party asserts that a trial was unfair due to legal errors that prejudiced its case.

MOTION FOR DIRECTED VERDICT: A request made by the defendant in a civil case. Asserts that the plaintiff has raised no genuine issue to be tried and asks the judge to rule in favor of the defense. This motion is typically made after the plaintiff is done presenting his or her case.

MOTION FOR SUMMARY JUDGMENT: A request made before a trial begins by one of the parties to a civil case. Asserts that no issues of material fact remain for resolution by a trial and one party is clearly entitled to judgment.

MOTION TO DISMISS: In a civil case, a request to a judge by the defendant, asserting that even if all the allegations are true, the plaintiff is not entitled to any legal relief and thus the case should be dismissed.

MOTION TO SUPPRESS EVIDENCE: A request to a judge to not admit evidence in a trial or hearing, often made when a party believes the evidence was unlawfully obtained.

NEGLIGENCE: A failure to use the degree of care that a reasonable person would use under the same circumstances.

NOTARY PUBLIC: A person authorized to witness the signing of documents.

OFFICERS OF A CORPORATION: Those people with day-to-day responsibility for running the corporation, such as the chief executive, chief financial officer, and treasurer.

OPINION: A witness's analysis, assessment, or judgment of something.

OWN RECOGNIZANCE: A person who promises to appear in court to answer criminal charges is allowed to be released on his or her 'own recognizance' and may be excused from paying any bail.

PAROLE: A system that provides for the supervised release of prisoners before their terms are over. Congress has abolished parole for people convicted of federal crimes.

PATENT: A document issued to an inventor by the United States Patent and Trademark Office. Contains a detailed description of what the invention is and how to make or use it and provides rights against infringers.

PENALTY PHASE: The second part of a bifurcated trial, in which the jury hears evidence and then votes on what penalty or damages to impose.

PEREMPTORY CHALLENGES: Limited number of challenges each side in a trial can use to eliminate potential jurors without stating a reason. These challenges may not be used to keep members of a particular race or sex off the jury.

PERJURY: A crime in which a person knowingly makes a false statement while under oath in court. In some jurisdictions, making a false statement in a legal document can also be considered perjury.

PERSONAL RECOGNIZANCE: Sometimes called own recognizance. A person who promises to appear in court to answer criminal charges can sometimes be released from jail without having to pay bail. This person is said to be released on his or her personal recognizance.

PERSONAL REPRESENTATIVE: A person who manages the legal affairs of another, such as a power of attorney or executor.

PETIT JURY: The jurors impaneled to hear a civil or criminal trial. It is distinguished from a grand jury.

PETITION: A written application to the court asking for specific action to be taken.

PLAINTIFF: The person who initiates a civil lawsuit.

PLEA BARGAIN: A negotiated agreement between the defense and the prosecution in a criminal case. Typically the defendant agrees to plead guilty to a specified charge in exchange for an oral promise of a lower sentence.

PLEADINGS: In a civil case, the allegations by each party of their claims and defenses.

POWER OF ATTORNEY: The authority to act legally for another person.

PRECEDENT: A previously decided case that is considered binding in the court where it was issued and in all lower courts in the same jurisdiction.

PRELIMINARY HEARING: Legal proceeding used in some states in which a prosecutor presents evidence to a judge in an attempt to show that there is probable cause that a person committed a crime. If the judge is convinced probable cause exists to charge the person, then the prosecution proceeds to the next phase. If not, the charges are dropped.

PREPONDERANCE OF THE EVIDENCE: The level of proof required to prevail in most civil cases. The judge or jury must be persuaded that the facts are more probably one way (the plaintiff's way) than another (the defendant's).

PRE-SENTENCING REPORT: A report prepared for a judge to assist in sentencing. It typically contains information about prior convictions and arrests, work history and family details.

PRIMA FACIE: Latin for "at first view." Refers to the minimum amount of evidence a plaintiff must have to avoid having a case dismissed. It is said that the plaintiff must make a prima facie case.

PRIVILEGED COMMUNICATION: Conversation that takes places within the context of a protected relationship, such as that between an attorney and client, a husband and wife, a priest and penitent, and a doctor and patient. The law often protects against forced disclosure of such conversations.

PROBABLE CAUSE: A reasonable belief that a person has committed a crime.

PROBATION: The release into the community of a defendant who has been found guilty of a crime, typically under certain conditions such as paying a fine, doing community service, or attending a drug treatment program. Violation of the conditions can result in incarceration. In the employment context, probation refers to the trial period some new employees go through.

PROMISSORY NOTE: A written document in which a borrower agrees (promises) to pay back money to a lender according to specified terms.

PROSECUTOR: The government lawyer who investigates and tries criminal cases. He is typically known as a district attorney, state's attorney, or United States attorney.

PROTECTIVE ORDER: In litigation, an order that prevents the disclosure of sensitive information except to certain individuals under certain conditions. In a domestic dispute this is an order that prevents one party from approaching another, often within a specified distance.

PUBLIC DEFENDER: A lawyer who works for a state or local agency representing clients accused of a crime who cannot afford to pay.

PUNITIVE DAMAGES: Money awarded to a victim that is intended to punish a defendant and stop the person or business from repeating the type of conduct that caused an injury. These damages are also intended to deter others from similar conduct.

QUASH: To nullify, void, or declare invalid.

QUID PRO QUO: Latin phrase that means 'what for what' or 'something for something.' It is the concept of getting something of value in return for giving something of value. For a contract to be binding, it usually must involve the exchange of something of value.

REAL PROPERTY: Land and all the things that are attached to it. Anything that is not real property is personal property and personal property is anything that isn't nailed down, dug into or built onto the land. A house is real property, but a dining room set is not.

REASONABLE CARE: The level of care a typical person would use if faced with the same circumstances.

REASONABLE DOUBT: The level of certainty a juror must have to find a defendant guilty of a crime.

RE-CROSS EXAMINATION: Questioning a witness about matters brought up during re-direct examination.

RE-DIRECT EXAMINATION: Questioning a witness about matters brought up during cross examination.

REMAND: When an appellate court sends a case back to a lower court for further proceedings.

REQUEST FOR PRODUCTION: A written request from one party to another for information or materials.

RETAINER: Refers to the up-front payment a client gives a lawyer or an expert witness to accept a case. The client is paying to "retain" the lawyer's services.

RIGHT AGAINST SELF-INCRIMINATION: Granted by the Fifth Amendment. This allows a person to refuse to answer questions that would subject him or her to accusation of a criminal act.

RULES OF EVIDENCE: The legislative rules that govern the determination of admissibility of evidence in dispute resolution.

SERVICE OF PROCESS: The act of notifying other parties that a legal case has been filed. It includes the steps they should take in order to respond.

SETTLEMENT: The resolution or compromise by the parties in a civil lawsuit.

SETTLEMENT AGREEMENT: In a civil lawsuit, the document that spells out the terms of an out-of-court compromise.

SLANDER: Defamatory (false and injurious) oral statements or gestures.

SOLE PROPRIETORSHIP: A form of business organization in which an individual is fully and personally liable for all the obligations (including debts) of the business, is entitled to all of its profits, and exercises complete managerial control.

SPOLIATION: The intentional or negligent withholding, hiding, alteration, or destruction of evidence.

STANDING: The legal right to initiate a lawsuit. To do so, a person must be sufficiently affected by the matter at hand, and there must be a case or controversy that can be resolved by legal action.

STATUTE: A law passed by any legislative body that governs people and activities in any locale or jurisdiction.

STATUTES OF LIMITATIONS: Laws setting deadlines for filing lawsuits within a certain time after events occur that are the source of a claim.

STRICT LIABILITY: Liability even when there is no proof of negligence. Often applicable in product liability cases against manufacturers who are legally responsible for injuries caused by defects in their products, even if they were not personally negligent.

SUBPOENA: An order compelling a person to appear to testify or produce documents.

SUMMARY JUDGMENT: See *Motion for Summary Judgment*.

SUMMATION: The closing argument in a trial.

SUMMONS: A legal document that notifies a party that a lawsuit has been initiated against them. It also states when and where the party must appear to answer the charges.

TANGIBLE PERSONAL PROPERTY: Anything other than real estate or money, including furniture, cars, jewelry, and china.

TESTIMONY: The presentation of evidence, observations, and opinions by witnesses to a judge or jury in a judicial hearing.

TITLE: Ownership of property.

TITLE SEARCH: A review of the land records to determine the ownership and description of the property.

TORT: A civil wrong that result in an injury to a person or property.

TRADEMARK: A word, name or symbol used to identify products sold or services provided by a business. A trademark distinguishes the products or services of one business from those of others in the same field. A business using a trademark has the right to prevent other businesses from using it and can get money to compensate for its infringement.

TRADE NAME: The name used to identify a business.

TRANSCRIPT: The written version of verbal testimony in a judicial hearing.

TRIAL: A hearing in the court system at which evidence is presented to the trier of fact to resolve a dispute.

TRIER OF FACT: A judge, jury, or other group of people who hear evidence in a dispute and make a determination to resolve the dispute.

TRUST: Property given to a trustee to manage for the benefit of a third person. Generally the beneficiary gets interest and dividends on the trust assets for a set number of years.

TRUSTEE: Person or institution that oversees and manages a trust.

VALID CLAIM: A grievance that can be resolved by legal action.

VERDICT: The formal decision issued by a jury on the issues of fact that were presented at trial.

VOIR DIRE: A French phrase that means "to speak the truth." This refers to the process of interviewing prospective jurors and expert witnesses, in order to determine their admissibility for their respective roles.

WARRANT: An official order authorizing a specific act, such as an arrest or the search of someone's home.

WARRANTY: A promise about a product made by either a manufacturer or a seller.

WITNESS: Person who comes to court and swears under oath to give truthful evidence.

WRIT: A judicial order

Appendix B

Federal Rules of Evidence
Opinions and Expert Testimony

Rule 701. Opinion Testimony by Lay Witnesses

If the witness is not testifying as an expert, the witness' testimony in the form of opinions or inferences is limited to those opinions or inferences which are (a) rationally based on the perception of the witness and (b) helpful to a clear understanding of the witness' testimony or the determination of a fact in issue, and (c) not based on scientific, technical, or other specialized knowledge within the scope of Rule 702.

Rule 702. Testimony by Experts

If scientific, technical, or other specialized knowledge will assist the trier of fact to understand the evidence or to determine a fact in issue, a witness qualified as an expert by knowledge, skill, experience, training, or education, may testify thereto in the form of an opinion or otherwise, if (1) the testimony is based upon sufficient facts or data, (2) the testimony is the product of reliable principles and methods, and (3) the witness has applied the principles and methods reliably to the facts of the case.

Rule 703. Bases of Opinion Testimony by Experts

The facts or data in the particular case upon which an expert bases an opinion or inference may be those perceived by or made known to the expert at or before the hearing. If of a type reasonably relied upon by experts in the particular field in forming opinions or inferences upon the subject, the facts or data need not be admissible in evidence in order for the opinion or inference to be admitted. Facts or data that are otherwise inadmissible shall not be disclosed to the jury by the proponent of the opinion or inference unless the court determines that their probative value in assisting the jury to evaluate the expert's opinion substantially outweighs their prejudicial effect.

Rule 704. Opinion on Ultimate Issue

(a) Except as provided in subdivision (b), testimony in the form of an opinion or inference otherwise admissible is not objectionable because it embraces an ultimate issue to be decided by the trier of fact.

(b) No expert witness testifying with respect to the mental state or condition of a defendant in a criminal case may state an opinion or inference as to whether the defendant did or did not have the mental state or condition constituting an element of the crime charged or of a defense thereto. Such ultimate issues are matters for the trier of fact alone.

Rule 705. Disclosure of Facts or Data Underlying Expert Opinion

The expert may testify in terms of opinion or inference and give reasons therefore without first testifying to the underlying facts or data, unless the court requires otherwise. The expert may in any event be required to disclose the underlying facts or data on cross-examination.

Rule 706. Court Appointed Experts

(a) Appointment.

The court may on its own motion or on the motion of any party enter an order to show cause why expert witnesses should not be appointed, and may request the parties to submit nominations. The court may appoint any expert witnesses agreed upon by the parties, and may appoint expert witnesses of its own selection. An expert witness shall not be appointed by the court unless the witness consents to act. A witness so appointed shall be informed of the witness' duties by the court in writing, a copy of which shall be filed with the clerk, or at a conference in which the parties shall have opportunity to participate. A witness so appointed shall advise the parties of the witness' findings, if any; the witness' deposition may be taken by any party; and the witness may be called to testify by the court or any party. The witness shall be subject to cross-examination by each party, including a party calling the witness.

(b) Compensation.

Expert witnesses so appointed are entitled to reasonable compensation in whatever sum the court may allow. The compensation thus fixed is payable from funds which may be provided by law in criminal cases and civil actions and proceedings involving just compensation under the Fifth Amendment. In other civil actions and proceedings the compensation shall be paid by the parties in such proportion and at such time as the court directs, and thereafter charged in like manner as other costs.

(c) Disclosure of appointment.

In the exercise of its discretion, the court may authorize disclosure to the jury of the fact that the court appointed the expert witness.

(d) Parties' experts of own selection.

Nothing in this rule limits the parties in calling expert witnesses of their own selection.

Appendix C

Federal Rules of Civil Procedure – Rule 26
Duty to Disclose
General Provisions Governing Discovery

(a) Required Disclosures.

(1) Initial Disclosures.

(A) In General. *Except as exempted by Rule 26(a)(1)(B) or as otherwise stipulated or ordered by the court, a party must, without awaiting a discovery request, provide to the other parties:*

(i) the name and, if known, the address and telephone number of each individual likely to have discoverable information — along with the subjects of that information — that the disclosing party may use to support its claims or defenses, unless the use would be solely for impeachment;

(ii) a copy — or a description by category and location — of all documents, electronically stored information, and tangible things that the disclosing party has in its possession, custody, or control and may use to support its claims or defenses, unless the use would be solely for impeachment;

(iii) a computation of each category of damages claimed by the disclosing party — who must also make available for inspection and copying as underRule 34 the documents or other evidentiary material, unless privileged or protected from disclosure, on which each computation is based, including materials bearing on the nature and extent of injuries suffered; and

(iv) for inspection and copying as under Rule 34, any insurance agreement under which an insurance business may be liable to satisfy all or part of a possible judgment in the action or to indemnify or reimburse for payments made to satisfy the judgment.

(B) Proceedings Exempt from Initial Disclosure. *The following proceedings are exempt from initial disclosure:*

(i) an action for review on an administrative record;

(ii) a forfeiture action in rem arising from a federal statute;

(iii) a petition for habeas corpus or any other proceeding to challenge a criminal conviction or sentence;

(iv) an action brought without an attorney by a person in the custody of the United States, a state, or a state subdivision;

(v) an action to enforce or quash an administrative summons or subpoena;

(vi) an action by the United States to recover benefit payments;

(vii) an action by the United States to collect on a student loan guaranteed by the United States;

(viii) a proceeding ancillary to a proceeding in another court; and

(ix) an action to enforce an arbitration award.

(C) Time for Initial Disclosures — In General. *A party must make the initial disclosures at or* within *14 days after the parties' Rule 26(f) conference unless a different time is set by stipulation or court order, or unless a party objects during the conference that initial disclosures are not appropriate in this action and states the objection in the proposed discovery plan. In ruling on the objection, the court must determine what disclosures, if any, are to be made and must set the time for disclosure.*

(D) Time for Initial Disclosures — For Parties Served or Joined Later. *A party that is first served or otherwise joined after the Rule 26(f) conference must make the initial disclosures within 30 days after being*

served or joined, unless a different time is set by stipulation or court order.

(E) Basis for Initial Disclosure; Unacceptable Excuses. *A party must make its initial disclosures based on the information then reasonably available to it. A party is not excused from making its disclosures because it has not fully investigated the case or because it challenges the sufficiency of another party's disclosures or because another party has not made its disclosures.*

(2) Disclosure of Expert Testimony.

(A) In General. *In addition to the disclosures required by Rule 26(a)(1), a party must disclose to the other parties the identity of any witness it may use at trial to present evidence under Federal Rule of Evidence 702, 703, or 705.*

(B) Written Report. *Unless otherwise stipulated or ordered by the court, this disclosure must be accompanied by a written report — prepared and signed by the witness — if the witness is one retained or specially employed to provide expert testimony in the case or one whose duties as the party's employee regularly involve giving expert testimony. The report must contain:*

(i) a complete statement of all opinions the witness will express and the basis and reasons for them;

(ii) the data or other information considered by the witness in forming them;

(iii) any exhibits that will be used to summarize or support them;

(iv) the witness's qualifications, including a list of all publications authored in the previous 10 years;

(v) a list of all other cases in which, during the previous 4 years, the witness testified as an expert at trial or by deposition; and

(vi) a statement of the compensation to be paid for the study and testimony in the case.

(C) Time to Disclose Expert Testimony. *A party must make these disclosures at the times and in the sequence that the court orders. Absent a stipulation or a court order, the disclosures must be made:*

(i) at least 90 days before the date set for trial or for the case to be ready for trial; or

(ii) if the evidence is intended solely to contradict or rebut evidence on the same subject matter identified by another party under Rule 26(a)(2)(B), within 30 days after the other party's disclosure.

(D) Supplementing the Disclosure. *The parties must supplement these disclosures when required under Rule 26(e).*

(3) Pretrial Disclosures.

(A) In General. *In addition to the disclosures required by Rule 26(a)(1) and (2), a party must provide to the other parties and promptly file the following information about the evidence that it may present at trial other than solely for impeachment:*

(i) the name and, if not previously provided, the address and telephone number of each witness — separately identifying those the party expects to present and those it may call if the need arises;

(ii) the designation of those witnesses whose testimony the party expects to present by deposition and, if not taken stenographically, a transcript of the pertinent parts of the deposition; and

(iii) an identification of each document or other exhibit, including summaries of other evidence — separately identifying those items the party expects to offer and those it may offer if the need arises.

(B) Time for Pretrial Disclosures; Objections. *Unless the court orders otherwise, these disclosures must be made at least 30 days before trial. Within 14 days after they are made, unless the court sets a different time, a party may serve and promptly file a list of the following objections: any objections to the use under Rule 32(a) of a deposition designated by another party under Rule 26(a)(3)(A)(ii); and any objection, together with the grounds for it, that may be made to the admissibility of materials identified under Rule 26(a)(3)(A)(iii). An objection not so made — except for one under Federal Rule of Evidence 402 or 403 — is waived unless excused by the court for good cause.*

(4) Form of Disclosures.

Unless the court orders otherwise, all disclosures under Rule 26(a) must be in writing, signed, and served.

<u>(b) Discovery Scope and Limits.</u>

(1) Scope in General.

Unless otherwise limited by court order, the scope of discovery is as follows: Parties may obtain discovery regarding any nonprivileged matter that is relevant to any party's claim or defense — including the existence, description, nature, custody, condition, and location of any documents or other tangible things and the identity and location of persons who know of any discoverable matter. For good cause, the court may order discovery of any matter relevant to the subject matter involved in the action. Relevant information need not be admissible at the trial if the discovery appears reasonably calculated to lead to the discovery of admissible evidence. All discovery is subject to the limitations imposed by Rule 26(b)(2)(C).

(2) Limitations on Frequency and Extent.

(A) When Permitted. *By order, the court may alter the limits in these rules on the number of depositions and interrogatories or on the length of depositions under Rule 30. By order or local rule, the court may also limit the number of requests under Rule 36.*

(B) Specific Limitations on Electronically Stored Information. *A party need not provide discovery of electronically stored information from sources that the party identifies as not reasonably accessible because of undue burden or cost. On motion to compel discovery or for a protective order, the party from whom discovery is sought must show that the information is not reasonably accessible because of undue burden or cost. If that showing is made, the court may nonetheless order discovery from such sources if the requesting party shows good cause, considering the limitations of Rule 26(b)(2)(C). The court may specify conditions for the discovery.*

(C) When Required. *On motion or on its own, the court must limit the frequency or extent of discovery otherwise allowed by these rules or by local rule if it determines that:*

(i) the discovery sought is unreasonably cumulative or duplicative, or can be obtained from some other source that is more convenient, less burdensome, or less expensive;

(ii) the party seeking discovery has had ample opportunity to obtain the information by discovery in the action; or

(iii) the burden or expense of the proposed discovery outweighs its likely benefit, considering the needs of the case, the amount in controversy, the parties' resources, the importance of the issues at stake in the action, and the importance of the discovery in resolving the issues.

(3) Trial Preparation: Materials.

(A) Documents and Tangible Things. *Ordinarily, a party may not discover documents and tangible things that are prepared in anticipation of litigation or for trial by or for another party or its representative (including the other party's attorney, consultant, surety, indemnitor, insurer, or agent). But, subject to Rule 26(b)(4), those materials may be discovered if:*

(i) they are otherwise discoverable under Rule 26(b)(1); and

(ii) the party shows that it has substantial need for the materials to prepare its case and cannot, without undue hardship, obtain their substantial equivalent by other means.

(B) Protection Against Disclosure. *If the court orders discovery of those materials, it must protect against disclosure of the mental impressions, conclusions, opinions, or legal theories of a party's attorney or other representative concerning the litigation.*

(C) Previous Statement. *Any party or other person may, on request and without the required showing, obtain the person's own previous statement about the action or its subject matter. If the request is refused, the person may move for a court order, and Rule 37(a)(5) applies to the award of expenses. A previous statement is either:*

(i) a written statement that the person has signed or otherwise adopted or approved; or

(ii) a contemporaneous stenographic, mechanical, electrical, or other recording — or a transcription of it — that recites substantially verbatim the person's oral statement.

(4) Trial Preparation: Experts.

(A) Expert Who May Testify. *A party may depose any person who has been identified as an expert whose opinions may be presented at trial. If Rule 26(a)(2)(B) requires a report from the expert, the deposition may be conducted only after the report is provided.*

(B) Expert Employed Only for Trial Preparation. *Ordinarily, a party may not, by interrogatories or deposition, discover facts known or opinions held by an expert who has been retained or specially employed by another party in anticipation of litigation or to prepare for trial and who is not expected to be called as a witness at trial. But a party may do so only:*

(i) as provided in Rule 35(b); or

(ii) on showing exceptional circumstances under which it is impracticable for the party to obtain facts or opinions on the same subject by other means.

(C) Payment. *Unless manifest injustice would result, the court must require that the party seeking discovery:*

(i) pay the expert a reasonable fee for time spent in responding to discovery under Rule 26(b)(4)(A) or (B); and

(ii) for discovery under (B), also pay the other party a fair portion of the fees and expenses it reasonably incurred in obtaining the expert's facts and opinions.

Appendix D

Sample Expert Report

Expert Report of Judd Robbins in Plaintiff v. Defendant

Case No. xx-yyyy

I, JUDD ROBBINS, DECLARE AS FOLLOWS:

I. Background and Qualifications

I have worked in the computer industry for more than forty years. I have extensive experience working with computer software and systems, using a variety of processor hardware as well as general and customized software, including operating systems, programming languages, and database management systems. I have programmed several name and address mailing systems for my own businesses and for other companies, and I have observed the data structures for several other such systems during my twenty years of litigation support experience and thirty five years of application system experience. A true and correct copy of my curriculum vitae, which contains education, experience, and publications, is attached hereto as Exhibit A. I have personal knowledge of the facts stated herein, and could testify to them if called up to do so.

I have been retained, and am recognized in both the United States and the United Kingdom, as an expert witness and/or consultant. Since 1986, I have been retained in more than 100 cases, specializing in computer forensics and intellectual property rights. These include computer related copyright, patent, and trademark infringement matters, as well as trade secret misappropriation analyses. I have testified roughly two dozen times out of the total cases in which I have been retained, the last four years of which are listed in Exhibit B.

I have three degrees:

- A Bachelor of Arts in Physics from Bowdoin College in Maine (1967).

- A Master of Science in Information and Control Science from the University of Michigan (1968).

- A Master of Arts in Computer Science from the University of California at Berkeley (1974).

II. Exhibits:

A. Current Curriculum Vitae of Judd Robbins.

B. Previous Testimony over the last four years.

C. U.S. Patent #6,272,495B1 by Sanington: Dated Aug 7,2001; Filed Apr 22,1998

D. ... Add lines here for other Exhibits that you create and attach.

III. Compensation: In this matter, I am being compensated for my time at the rate of $450.00/hour plus expenses.

IV. Address: My current address is 422 Main Street Suite B, Ashland, OR 97520 and my business phone number is 949-666-5030.

V. The data or other information I considered:

- Plaintiff's First Amended Complaint.

- Plaintiff's Supplemental List of Claims to be asserted at Trial.

- Defendant's Reply to Plaintiff's List of Claims to be asserted at Trial.

- Expert Report and Supplemental Expert Report of James R. Baker, Ph.D. with exhibits referenced in the report.

- ... Add lines here for other information that you considered.

VI Methodology Used and Procedures Followed:
I had a preliminary conference call on April 7, 2006 with Dan Millman and James Baker to discuss this case and my interest/availability. On April 14, 2006, I was retained as an expert consultant in this matter. After signing a retainer agreement and a non-disclosure agreement, I began to receive and review miscellaneous printed and electronic information (as listed above in Section V).

... Continue here with appropriate descriptions for your work in the case.

VII Conclusions Reached, the Basis for Them, and Opinions To Be Expressed:

There is no apparent 'trade secret' in Defragger that could even be misappropriated. Both Expert Reports focus largely on allegedly copied versions of source code from the 2001 time frame, as well as contents of a Patent Application ("patent") filed by James Baker (Exhibit O). The concepts seen in the SuperDuper source code reveal nothing that was not already either public knowledge, or general knowledge known in the mail list service industry. The Defragger source code provided no competitive advantage to Plaintiff. Before 2001, other programs like Second Life' TweakTop (see Exhibit F) that were already competitively available, offered alternative comparison and merging logic. Other companies (see Exhibit C) that are currently in business and offer competitive defragmentation services and/or software have been in business since the mid-1970's and have employed all of, and often much more than, the techniques seen in the Defragger source code from Plaintiff.

Additional Opinions, explanations, foundation, references, documentation ...

DATED, [today's date] in the State of Oregon, County of Jackson

Signature Here......

Judd Robbins

Appendix E

Sample Fee Schedule
and Retainer Agreement

This letter sets forth the general terms of the expert witness and consulting services of Presentation Dynamics, including its fees and billing policies and procedures. Retention will occur after both parties sign this Agreement and we receive the initial retainer fee.

1. You will be charged our prevailing rates for time spent on your matter, according to the level of service, regardless of the nature of the service (travel, analysis, testimony, etc). The hourly rate for Judd Robbins is $395, for any Associate is $200, and for any Administrative Assistant is $50. When your case involves work away from our offices (depositions, trials, meetings, long travel days, etc.), we will bill at our normal rates, subject to a calendar day minimum charge of eight hours. Billings for our work will be submitted at reasonable intervals, are payable to Presentation Dynamics on receipt, and must be paid prior to deposition or trial testimony. Non-payment after 15 days will be subject to a retroactive interest charge of 1.5%/month on the total invoice. Our rates may be adjusted from time to time, but no more than once a year, and therefore are subject to change during the course of a lengthy engagement. In addition, we charge separately for travel expenses and occasional non-trivial additional equipment, administrative, or support expenses (couriers, graphic artists, etc.).

2. You agree to pay the amounts stated on each billing invoice within 15 days of your receipt of the statement. If we have to retain a

lawyer or collection service to collect unpaid invoices, you agree to be responsible for your own as well as our incurred legal and/or collection service charges. In the event of any disputes arising from this Agreement, you agree that this Agreement shall be deemed to have been entered into in the state of Oregon and its validity, construction, and legal effects shall be governed by the laws of the state of Oregon, applicable to agreements made therein, and to be performed therein.

3. To formally retain Presentation Dynamics for this new consulting assignment, we require an initial retainer fee of $5,000. This retainer will be applied to the last invoice we render to you. Occasionally, we may require an increase in the amount of the retainer, depending on your payment history or on the scope of work, and we reserve the right to do so. All retainer amounts are deposited into our general account and are refundable, without interest, to the extent not applied against invoices as aforesaid. Some cases require commitment of significantly more initial time on our part as well as some advance dollar expenditures for travel. Prior to beginning or continuing such services, we may need to agree on and we may need to receive the agreed-upon retainer amount. Required retainer payments may be done by electronic wire transfer or by company check; the initial retainer payment includes a $1000 sum that represents a non-refundable minimum fee for services. The entire amount of the retainer is applicable to all charges, and any unused portion of the retainer is refundable on closure of the assignment/case. You may not designate Presentation Dynamics, Judd Robbins, or any of its consultants for your case without our permission. The retainer may need to be replenished from time to time in order to assure prepayment of large blocks of time that we may be required to schedule on your behalf.

If you have any additional questions, please call me. If you decide to retain Presentation Dynamics, we can then discuss further plans, as well as arrange for the retainer, and we can begin helping you with this matter. If your decision takes more than a week from the date of this page, we would need to discuss our schedule and availability once again before we can commit to taking on your case. If the above terms meet with your approval and you wish us to proceed with providing you with expert witness and consulting services in accordance with such terms, please complete and mail or fax back a signed copy of this letter, together with the requested retainer.

Please do not hesitate to call me if you have any questions regarding this letter. I appreciate your decision to select us to provide you with computer services, and we're looking forward to working with you on this case.

Sincerely,	Case Identifier: _____
	Terms Accepted by:
Judd Robbins	Name (Please Print): _____
	Name (Please Sign): _____
	Firm Name: _____
	Date: _____

Appendix F - Sample 3-Fold CV

JUDD ROBBINS
Computer Specialist

2305-C Ashland Street #437
Ashland, OR 97520
Phone: (541) 512-2508 PST
Fax: (949) 666-5030
Email: judd@juddrobbins.com
http://www.juddrobbins.com

M.A. Computer Science (UC Berkeley)
M.S. Information Science (U. of Michigan)
Expert Witness in Software Analysis
40+ Years International Experience:
Analysis and Programming
Seminar Design and Presentation
Customized Training in IBM Software
Starring in over 25 Videos and DVDs
Best Selling Author of 30 Computer Books

Litigation Support
- Expert Witness/Consultant since 1986
- Specializing in *intellectual property, computer forensics, Internet.*
- Member: Forensic Association of Computer Technologists.

Business
- President, Presentation Dynamics 9/93 - Present.
- Owner/President, Computer Options, 8/82 - 9/93.
- MIS Manager, Education Manager, Operating Systems Specialist, Data General Corp., 5/78 - 8/82
- Patient Systems Programming Manager and Supervisor, Senior Systems Programmer/Analyst, Kaiser Foundation Hospitals, 1/75 - 5/78
- Programmer/Analyst, Hewlett-Packard (Medical Electronics Division), 1/73 - 8/73; and 4/70 - 8/71
- Research Scientist, Erasmus University (Appointment to the Medical Faculty), 8/71 - 1/73

Research
- Computer simulation — Heartbeat modeling
- Data analysis and reduction — Ballistocardiography
- Data capture/conversion — Real time monitoring
- Data communications — Electromagnetic induction
- 3D Probability calculations — Missile interception

Education
- UC Berkeley: M.A. Computer Science, '74
- University of Michigan: M.S. Info/Ctrl Science, '68
- Bowdoin College: B.A. Physics, '67

Presentations
- Cable TV Specials for MSNBC, Court TV, and Tech TV — As computer forensics expert, and as 'Cyber Sleuth'
- POST-certified Forensics seminars for Law Enforcement.
- State-certified Computer Forensics seminars for lawyers.
- Society of Forensic Engineers and Scientists — Internet for Specialists
- National Forensic Center — Using the Internet for Lawyers and Experts
- International Law Forum on Strategies for Expert Witnesses
- American/Canadian Medical Associations — Health Care Computing
- American Educational Organizations — Computers in Education
- Lecturer: UC Berkeley; UC Santa Cruz; San Jose State ; SF State
- Public Seminar Leader (U.S., Canada, Great Britain) — Internet and PC software subjects
- Private seminars to major U.S. organizations — AT&T, IBM, US Navy, Scott Paper, Dupont, TRW, & others

Computers
- **Internet**: Website programming and domain server hosting
- **Mainframes**: IBM & CDC
- **Minis**: DGC, HP, DEC
- **Micros**: PCs &compatibles
- **Software**: Data Base, Spreadsheet, Word Processing, Graphics, Computer-Aided Design, Communications, Operating Systems, CICS, Networking, Desktop publishing, Assembler, dBASE, SQL, Visual Basic, Fortran, Pascal, Basic, COBOL , C, C++, Algol, HTML, Java, Javascript, PSP, Jquery, PL/1, CGI, Perl, Flash

Licenses and Certifications
- Real Estate Broker's License — Massachusetts
- American Council on Exercise — Instructor certifications in Group Fitness and Fitness Yoga
- Jujitsu America - Black Belt
- YogaFit – Certified Yoga Instructor
- Physical Mind Institute – Certified Pilates Instructor

Appendix G

Index